the pull
of moving water

Other Books in the
Washington State University Press
Memoirs Series

the *pull*
of moving water

Alice Koskela

Illustrations by Stephanie Inman

WSU
PRESS

Washington State University Press
Pullman, Washington

Washington State University Press
PO Box 645910
Pullman, Washington 99164-5910
Phone: 800-354-7360 FAX: 509-335-8568
email: wsupress@wsu.edu
www.publications.wsu.edu/wsupress
© 1999 by the Board of Regents of Washington State University
All rights reserved
First printing 1999

Chapter One previously appeared in a slightly different version in the 1990 Idaho Centennial Edition of the Boise State University literary magazine *cold-drill*.

Illustrations are by Stephanie Inman. Illustrations are copyrighted by Alice Koskela, who has granted permission to WSU Press for their use in this book.

Library of Congress Cataloging-in-Publication Data

Koskela, Alice, 1949–
    The pull of moving water / Alice Koskela.
        p.   cm. — (Washington State University Press memoirs series)
    ISBN 0-87422-180-3
    1. Koskela, Alice, 1949–   —Childhood and youth. 2. Emmett Region (Idaho) Biography. 3. Emmett Region (Idaho)—Social life and customs. 4. Farm life—Idaho—Emmett Region. 5. United States—Social life and customs—1945–1970. I. Title. II. Series.
F754.E46K67   1999
979.6'27—dc21   99–14948
    [B]   CIP

Contents

Arthur Eli Koskella
December 24, 1918–May 2, 1999
In loving memory

Acknowledgments

A BOOK IS A JOINT EFFORT. Other people provide information you couldn't get anywhere else. They take time to read what you write and tell you what they really think. They encourage you when all there is is some words on white paper which may or may not ever make it to print. They tell you that what you're doing is important, that it matters. These are just some of those people to whom I am grateful.

Margot Knight, who urged me to think of myself as a writer. Cheryl Gratton, who always believed I could do it, even as I wasted years; and Kathy Barnard, whose friendship and encouragement are a source of joy to me. Clareene Wharry, who listened patiently and helped me see the humor in my mini-tragedies.

Keith Petersen, who patiently took this manuscript in bits and pieces and kept me working on it. Dale Goble and Dennis Colson, who allowed me to add to their reading stacks with pages entirely unrelated to law school. Cort Conley, who teaches by example how to live and write at the same time.

Arthur, who gave me a good reason to write this all down.

And Rudy, whose love keeps me going.

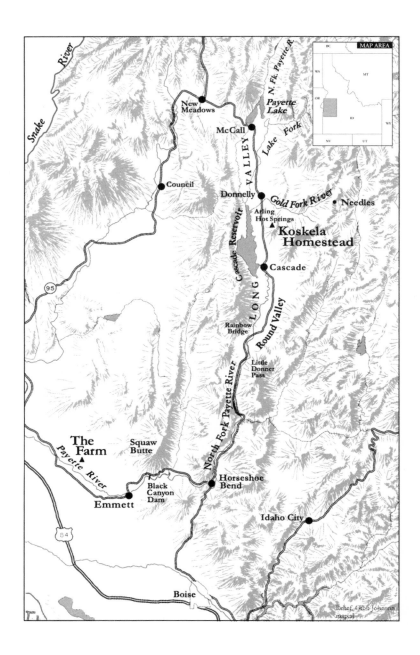

Preface

I GREW UP ON A FARM IN IDAHO in the 1950s, which is to say I felt trapped in the calm dead center of a storm, excitement swirling all around me, nothing happening at home. Occasionally someone or something would blow in from the outside: migrant workers from Mexico or transients from Tennessee or atomic fallout from Nevada. Television teased me with scenes from the world beyond the brown foothills that filled my horizon. *I Love Lucy, American Bandstand, The Lone Ranger, The Little Rascals* gave me glimpses of what it must be like out there, where lots of people actually lived in the same building, or you could get *this close* to Frankie Avalon or Dion singing their latest hits, or spend your days on horseback in the Real West, or have a whole gang of kids close by to play with every day. I was lonely and envious and impatient, wanting nothing more than out.

I could not appreciate serene summer mornings, the lilting calls of meadowlarks, or low cooing of mourning doves hanging in the still air. I could not appreciate living on a road that nobody else traveled; if we saw a car coming, it was coming *here.* I could not appreciate waking up because I wasn't tired anymore, not because a neighbor's noise pierced my sleep. I could not appreciate a father who could fix practically anything with what he happened to have in the shop, who wore the same overalls and shirts day after day, his only extravagance his White work boots, who came in after dark exhausted from irrigating and milking and in the summer from combining for other farmers, his face black with grain chaff and grease and dust. I could not appreciate my mother's persistence at writing, was a little embarrassed actually by her pieces in the newspaper about her own childhood or our farm family life, but without the dirt and smell of greasy hamburger cooking or our harsh words or sullen silence. I did not realize that she was wishing in her writing for something else, something cleaner and happier than what we had. If she made my father more articulate, if their conversations were more loving than any I had ever heard, if the house she described was immaculate and her children obedient and kind, what was that but a way to stand the dust and monotony and constant anxiety about money that defined our farm life?

But being a child means lacking the ability or inclination to see your parents as people, to recognize their sadness and longing and resignation. They must be your perfect and all-powerful protectors, and you will brook no flaws, no weakness. It is too terrifying.

One

1949-1955: IRRIGATION

THE CANAL WOUND around forty miles of dry Idaho foothills, last artery of a vascular system dispensing something like blood to our farm. Our ditches divided and redivided into smaller and smaller channels, trickling finally into capillary corrugates no wider than my hand. What was left of the water after it ran through fertilized corn fields and thirsty hay fields and smelly barnyards converged again in vein drain ditches returning their spent and despoiled contents to the river.

The canal was our lifeline. More than the highway or telephone wires, we needed what it carried. Our seasons were determined not by the calendar but by whether water flowed in the ditch. Watching it roll down the dry canal bed for the first time each spring felt almost religious. In the fall, some unseen hand miles away shut us off, leaving only a few shrinking puddles. The exposed, cracked canal bottom in winter somehow scared me; I kept my eyes on the sky when I rode my horse across the bridge and up into the foothills on cold grey days. The horse's hooves echoed hollow on planks holding us high above nothing.

The canal without water was a gash in the hillside, a reminder that we were intruders here, like the time my father's plow turned up a smooth stone bowl—sliced it in half, actually. My father stopped and got off his tractor and stood in the muddy field, holding the two halves in his big grimy farmer hands, touching something last touched by someone who never imagined him or the tractor belching diesel smoke or the shiny chrome plow catching his curved reflection as he stood trying to fit the pieces together. Screaming seagulls swarmed above him, hungry for field mice that tumbled helplessly from the freshly turned earth.

I found my first arrowhead in the barren foothills beyond the reach of the Bureau of Reclamation. I could ride across the canal bridge, open one gate, and lose myself. Back there the brown hills closed in around me like another time. The only sounds were wind and the horse's hooves breaking through dry grass and the saddle creaking beneath me. I could be gone for hours, dreaming about cowboys and cattle drives, wishing I lived in the real West, an exciting black-and-white place I knew only from the flickering scenes on television.

I was out farther than ever the day my horse stopped suddenly at the edge of a gully too wide for him to jump and too steep to walk down. The sun came out from behind a cloud just then, and I saw that the gully was littered with flint flashing like black diamonds. I jumped off, stumbled down the steep slope, and picked up a perfect arrowhead—I knew it was perfect because I could see all the ones the craftsman had discarded, the broken pieces of glassy black rock half chipped away and tossed aside because the angle was wrong or the chip too deep. Down there, below the wind, I stood in the middle of the ancient's workshop, a hidden place washed out by rain and revealed to me on that day only. I never found it again, although I looked for months afterward, like a prospector searching for the lost mother lode. For some reason I took just that one perfect arrowhead, sharp and smooth and warming in my hand while my horse found our way home.

My favorite place on the farm was a big dry hill that rose stubbornly out of an irrigated pasture. Up there the hard dirt grew only useless cheat grass; the hilltop had become a junkyard for broken down and obsolete farm machinery. I perched on the greying remains of a wooden-wheeled wagon, squinting into the distance. If I kept my eyes on the tawny foothills at the horizon, ignoring the sea of cultivated green below, it was easy to imagine: I was driving the lead team, whipping imaginary horses through dangerous territory, ever watchful for marauding Indians. When they attacked I grabbed my invisible rifle, shooting back and muttering "*kew! kew!*"—the child's universally recognized sound of gunfire.

My game would last until I was distracted by the loud snorts of our Holstein milk cows, a ridiculous audience with big eyes and dripping nostrils, drawn to the base of the hill by this strange commotion. Sometimes I would pretend they were buffalo and try to pick off one or two—*kew!*—but they wouldn't fall down or run away or even get closer so I might hit them with a dirt clod. The herd stood right at the pasture's edge, refusing to cross the little ditch that divided green grass from barren ground, soft from hard, food from not-food. Their big stupid faces finally made me laugh.

I spent most of my time alone, riding in the foothills or wandering our fields and crawling under barbed wire fences, careful not to brush against the ones that were "hot." I remember my first lesson in electricity, taught before I was old enough for school but fearless enough to explore the pastures with just a cow dog for company.

"Come here," my father said, beckoning me to a fence with round red insulators nailed to the posts. I could hear a faint buzz along the wire: those were the days before pulsating current, when the relentless jolt of an electric fence would send even a big calf bawling for its mother.

He held a pair of rubber-handled pliers in one hand and kept me at a safe distance with the other. The pliers clamped down. Little bolts of lightning jumped and crackled where the metal teeth held the wire, a miniature, menacing storm. He pulled the pliers back, and the faint odor of hot metal hung in the air.

"That's what will happen to your hand if you touch a hot wire," he warned. It was the only lesson I ever needed about electric fences.

My brother learned the rules of conductivity the hard way. It was late summer, we were bored, and on a dull hot afternoon we wandered to the edge of our irrigation pond, throwing rocks and sticks at the electric fence strung across one end of it to keep the cattle out. We stood barefoot in the shallow water, intent on our mindless game. Presently a foolish idea floated into my head. "Look at me!" I said, and laid a long stick on the humming wire.

Steve gasped, then stared in amazement at my ability to touch the deadly fence. I held the stick there a few moments before I tossed it in the pond.

"I'm magic," I smiled.

He knotted his toddler's brow.

"I'm magic too!" he cried, splashing through the pond. He grabbed the wire with both hands.

Standing there in the muddy water, his pudgy fingers clenching the fence, my brother opened his mouth in a soundless cry. His eyes grew wide with fear and pain but he didn't move. The electric current held him fast.

I stumbled in, wrapped my arms around his waist and pulled him off, nearly dragging the wire along with us as I staggered back to dry ground.

For a long time we just looked at each other. The sky was still a brilliant blue, red-winged blackbirds still sang riotously in the cattails, a warm wind still bent the weeds at our feet, just like before. My father kept hammering on something in his shop, my mother was hanging clothes on the line. I saw and heard the world go on just as it was, but brighter and louder somehow. We were both breathing hard.

He didn't cry, but held up his hands: a red line ran across his palms.

"Don't ever do that again," I whispered fiercely.

He shook his head.

"And don't tell anybody."

He never did.

The farm was my schoolroom before I was forced inside. I spent hours lying in the soft pasture grass, watching clouds form and re-form in fat silhouettes. I learned which way the killdeer's nest really was when she fluttered her phony broken wing and tried to lure me away, and knew not to touch the tiny brown speckled eggs in the nest I found camouflaged in the grass. I learned by watching my horse's eyes for just the right moment to bring my hand from behind my back and grab for his halter. Learned, riding, to watch his ears prick up or lay back flat or just take casual flicking notice of a sound.

Learned by watching men working in the hay how a stack is built, with the big wooden derrick and its thick wire cable creaking and the giant boom dipping and swinging like the ruined mast of a landlocked ship. And the Jackson fork at the end of the cable, its curved teeth big enough for men to sit on, a metal monster's mouth biting four bales of hay and taking them up, up until a man on top of the stack yells "tur-ip!" and somebody at the bottom pulls the trip rope and the bales drop off the fork with a thud. If it's too soon they drop too far and bounce and the stackers have to jump back. A good stacker waits until just the right moment and a good tripper can feel the right moment in the tension of the rope even though he can't see the top of the stack or the man at the other end trying to position the bales just right.

If they're good-natured stackers I get to ride out to the field on the slip—called that because it slips along the ground, a wooden land raft really, easier to load than wagons and much more fun for a kid to ride. I stand balancing on one board, then another as the tractor pulls the slip fast over the dips and swells of the earth, feeling the boards curve and straighten beneath my feet, careful not to fall off or I'll be left behind. The dirt road has been pounded to powder by the heavy slip and the big tractor wheels, and we slice through floury dust like a sleigh, I imagine, through snow. I close my eyes and hear the tractor snort, a prancing team.

In the field the men sink their curved hayhooks into hundred-pound bales and toss them easily on the slip, row upon row until the tractor driver has to shift down and the slip boards creak beneath the weight. We sit high on the prickly bales and the hot wind dries the sweaty faces of the haymen. I can still smell the sweet hay and the sweat and the diesel smoke from the tractor, still feel the bales shifting as the slip bends to the contours of the world.

All afternoon the big stack grows. In the last red of the sunset the last four bales swing up higher and higher and the derrick pole is poised at an impossible angle and the stackers hold out their arms to catch the fork and position it to fit those last bales in and for a moment everything stops because this is it. The men and the big fork and the bales are black against the red sky and everyone is looking up, waiting for the final "tur-ip!" when the bales drop neatly into the last space. The stackers wipe their foreheads with their forearms and take a last ride down to the ground on the monster teeth, swinging their legs in the air like schoolchildren, looking over their shoulders at the huge skyscraping stack they have built of bales.

Sitting across the road where I can see best, I'm hugging my knees and petting the dog and watching so hard I almost don't remember to jump on the empty slip when it passes by for the final ride to the house.

I started school already reading seed sacks and the names of pickups embossed on their tailgates and the gauges on our John Deere green and Massey Ferguson red tractors. I could write, too, a sort of legible longhand, learned by watching my mother and practiced in her lipstick on the bedroom walls, one incentive for getting me into first grade early. My birthday was late in September, past the deadline, but Mother convinced the teacher to let me take a "readiness test." I missed only one question—about the best place to store hay. We didn't get enough winter to need a hay barn, but the test was written by some Midwestern university professor, so I answered wrong with "stack."

I was allowed then to suffer through dull idyllic Dick and Jane readers and fill my tablet pages with up-and-down lines and circling loops so I could someday learn to print. The first week I peed my pants because I was too scared to ask to go to the bathroom. The teacher made me squat, mortified, over a heat register to dry.

Our school was called "Hanna" for some homesteader's daughter, a girl who came to the valley before Black Canyon Dam plugged the Payette River and made a big flat reservoir far upstream from our farm. At the time I never thought of Hanna as a girl, anymore than I could have imagined the farm gone back to wild dryland grass where deer wintered.

Hanna seemed like a huge building then. It was hip-roofed in a style popular in the twenties, orange stuccoed over the original clapboard with a big bell tower that made it look more like a mission church than a country schoolhouse. There were three classrooms for eight grades, a wide center stairway, and a big cold basement with a gymnasium and stage for plays and school dances and graduation ceremonies. A pitted concrete slab in front was a good place to roller-skate if you could dodge the big boys playing basketball. I skated until my knees were scabbed over and my backside bruised purple from too many hard landings. The ching-ching of metal skate wheels on rough cement was my recess music, syncopated by the slap of a basketball and the thung! of a rimshot bouncing back.

In first grade I had a violent crush on a red-haired boy named Rex Lee, the ditchrider's son. His face was spattered with rust-colored freckles, and his eyebrows and eyelashes were orange. Rex's father drove a battered green Ford pickup and was rumored to carry a shotgun on his daily inspections of the head-gates along the canal bank. He knew which concrete portals were supposed to be open, letting precious water down the ditches, and which ones to keep chained and padlocked shut. Rex bragged that he got to ride with his father sometimes, and that he had seen chains wrenched apart, padlocks smashed. It was just like rob-bery, his dad said.

Rex was a fifth grader, so old that I had no hope of being his girlfriend. But sometimes after school, while we waited for the bus, he would tickle me until I was shrieking and breathless, and this was enough. In the back of my Big Chief penmanship tablet I drew a lopsided heart with an arrow through it and our names inside, joined with a plus sign.

My first grade performance was uneven. However well I read, I couldn't color inside the lines, and I was clumsy with the dull rounded scissors we used to cut out construction paper pumpkins and turkey fan tails and folded snow flakes, and I just wanted to go home on the afternoon of the class Christmas party.

My teacher frowned but called my father and even let me wait outside on the big concrete steps while the others stayed in to sing carols and exchange gifts and eat sticky hard candy from brown paper sacks. A rare and perfect snowstorm swirled around me. I huddled happily in the soft windblown flakes, watching them blanket the bumpy cement walk and the empty fields be-yond. In this beautiful white quiet I waited until my father's car turned into the school yard, tires crunching in the snow. His headlights tunneled through the storm, illuminating each danc-ing crystal. Even the car motor was hushed, muffled by the damp downy air. I jumped up and ran joyfully through the deepening snow to the door he threw open for me.

I remember that storm because Christmases on the farm were hardly ever white. Snow was rare; that was why my father sold his high mountain ranch and brought my mother and me to the "lower country." He was tired of fighting long blizzard-buried winters, tired of waking on late summer mornings to find his clover crop ruined by freak frosts, tired of always losing to the cold. Luckily I was a sickly baby—another good reason to leave.

When spring finally came he drove down the canyon carved by the North Fork of the Payette, following the frothing river until it became a placid pool behind a dam. And then the river was forced to follow him, in canals and ditches and corrugates creating new farmland, feeding new dreams.

The author and her mother at the Lakefork ranch, winter 1950

The author at the Emmett farm, spring 1951

Two

1956: Heights

S O WE LIVED IN THE HOT, dry lower country, our irrigated farmland bordering on irredeemable desert. The Payette River began a hundred miles north and two thousand feet above us, flowing out of a deep cold lake and meandering through Long Valley, the forested haven we had to abandon (the story became) because I was a fragile infant and almost died that first winter. Moving was thus my fault. The river and its sapphire lake source were both named for a French fur trapper who tramped through the Idaho mountains and married several Indian wives before descending into civilization at Fort Boise, but I knew nothing of that Frenchman; Payette was simply the lake we left behind and the river we followed down to a farm on the sagebrushy edge of hell.

I wasn't yet a year old when we moved, but I learned by heart how my mother first saw our new place. We drove down the canyon in the early spring, as soon as the roads were cleared, turning west with the river at Horseshoe Bend. All she knew was that our farm was on the other side of Emmett. We didn't take the turn-off into town, but stayed on the state highway, passing nicely kept brick and stucco farmhouses, sturdy barns, and neat corrals in the background.

Is that it? she asked expectantly. *No,* my father said, *not yet.* The farther they went the worse the houses looked, and yet he kept driving, his big hands clenching the steering wheel, worried now she wouldn't like it. The highway ended and we turned onto a county road that ran to the base of some dry foothills and veered west again. Finally he slowed, easing the car onto a narrow rutted lane that appeared to end in the middle of a field. When my mother saw the tiny house she gasped.

Our house in Long Valley was surrounded by pine trees. My mother loved the hush of the wind in the heavy branches, the screeching hawks overhead, the splashing of Lakefork Creek outside the door. She didn't mind seven foot snow drifts or the late spring frosts or the blizzards that rattled the windows. Long Valley was so green and so clean. But when my father decided to move there was just no stopping him. Without even asking he sold their place and bought this awful little farm with no yard and just a few gnarled locust trees for shade, muddy fields stretching out in all directions. Magpies croaked in the spidery black locust branches. The empty ditch behind the house was just a slash in the ground. An unpainted outhouse announced the lack of a bathroom. *How could you do this!* my mother wailed, and her tears set me to crying too. My father jumped out of the car and pulled a cigarette from his coat pocket. He smoked furiously, seeing the ramshackle house and ugly bare trees and humiliating outhouse through her eyes. Finally he crushed his cigarette in the dirt and went back to the car, chewing on his lower lip. He opened the door for her.

It looks better on the inside, he said, but his voice made it a question. *I'll build an indoor bathroom right away. You'll see. It won't be so bad.*

My mother relived that day almost every time we drove home from town, until I could imagine it all clearly, the long dreary drive, her growing impatience and excitement. *There*, she would say, pointing to the Cruickshanks' white stucco house, with a pond and a red barn like in some child's story book, *that's where I thought we would live. Or there* (the Hansens' big brick house with fireplace on one end) *or there* (the Bradshaws' yellow bungalow with its front porch swing and lilac bushes on each side). All the places that weren't ours. Her eyes would narrow, seeing back to that day, and she would shake her head in disgust. By the time we finally turned down our lane I knew how ugly and forlorn our house was, even with the bathroom and two bedrooms my father added on, and the juniper and lilac bushes he planted next to the concrete sidewalks he poured, and the rail fence he built around the bumpy lawn. It would never be good enough.

At least we could visit Long Valley, in the summer when the heat was unbearable on the farm and my father could get someone to do the milking. We would spend a whole day and a night at my grandfather's homestead place. We always called it "*the* ranch," the way my Mormon classmates referred to their religion as "*the* church." It was a real ranch: two thousand acres of meadow and timber owned by my uncles Oscar and Jake. I loved driving to the ranch on a hot July morning, the road rising out of the dry foothills where only locust trees and cottonwoods grew, rising with the river up the canyon, being the first to spy a pine tree on a steep ridge, then another and another until soon we were winding through a real forest and the air rushing in our open car windows was cool and fresh off the frothing river.

Finally we would cross Rainbow Bridge, a graceful concrete arch on all the tourist postcards, and climb out onto the first valley floor. This was Round Valley, followed by Long Valley, names so dull and plain for such beautiful high meadows, ringed by range upon shadowy mountain range reaching back into the distance. By the time we turned up a gravel road at the "Koskela Bros." sign I could hardly wait, straining to see the white two-story house my grandfather built after my father and his sister Anna burned their first one to the ground, playing with matches. There was a big red barn and behind it a one-room bunkhouse, just like on the TV westerns. I could almost smell the leather saddles and bridles in the tackroom, almost feel the prickly hay in the loft. And of course there was the family graveyard on the hill behind the house.

Aunt Rose, Jake's wife, would come out to greet us, wiping her hands on her apron. Jake and Oscar were usually out working somewhere, moving cattle or irrigating clover or cutting their thin grassy hay. They were very rich and notoriously stingy. When they came to hunt pheasants on the farm they might stay a week or more and never even offer to buy groceries. For Christmas Oscar would sometimes send a box of Idaho Spud candy bars, turdish-looking chocolate mounds. I preferred Hersheys with almonds. Oscar was the oldest of my father's eight brothers. He was short and wiry and bow-legged from riding horses so much, and he had no use for children. Even though he was usually gruff with me, I loved to hear him talk. Oscar had the strongest accent of all my Finnish relatives, a clipped musical voice so much more interesting than the flat Idaho drawl I heard every day. Oscar never got married—my mother said he didn't want to pay for the license. Jake married Rose when she was teaching his little brothers and sisters in the country school a few miles from the ranch. Jake was tall and had just one good eye, the other milky and blind, ruined by an explosion in the schoolhouse stove when he was a boy. There were two versions of the story—that another boy put a bullet in the stove and Jake tried to get it out, or that Jake put the bullet in, and it went off before he could close the door. I preferred the second story; it was like the one about my father and Aunt Anna lighting their bedroom curtains on fire because they liked to watch the flames. It pleased me to hear how adults had misbehaved.

Out of the car at last, I would race up the hill to the giant stride my uncles had pilfered from the country school when it closed years before. It was a wonderful contraption—a combination trapeze and merry-go-round made from a tall steel pole with pairs of chains dangling from a wheel at the top. Three round wooden handles connected each pair of chains, one above another like rungs on a floating ladder. The wood had been rubbed smooth by hundreds of clutching hands, by children who were grown or even dead now holding on tight as their feet left the ground, screaming in delight. The giant stride was anchored deep in concrete on the hill behind the ranch house. It was a perfect place: I could take a running leap at the top and swing way out, soaring high over Aunt Rose's terraced rock garden, her strawberry plants, the broken concrete steps leading up the hill, and finally the blindingly bright metal of the ranch house roof, my knees bent up against my chest, gripping the wooden handle like death. If I ran fast enough and lifted off at just the right moment, it felt like I might fling myself out into the sky and just keep going. The trapeze chains clanged against the pole in the slightest breeze, a silvery tinkling music and the promise of flight.

The ranch was in the shadow of the Needles, five towering rock spires that jutted out of a mountain ridge, visible from just about anywhere in the valley, dark and ominous. There were herds of elk and deer around the Needles, and my father and Jake and Oscar and their younger brother Raymond went hunting there every year and got lost every time.

That was the thing about the Needles, you got turned around somehow up there, and even though you could look down and see the ranch and the ribbon of state highway crossing Long Valley, could almost hear the cars on the road, you couldn't seem to find your way down. The hunters would drag in long after dark with new getting lost stories to tell.

In Aunt Rose's bright kitchen they would sit and drink coffee to warm up, laughing and shaking their heads and talking about how they thought they were walking downhill, following Fool Hen Creek or some other stream off the mountain, and then they'd realize they weren't going down at all. *We walked and walked and walked and it seemed like we were headed home, and pretty soon we saw the same rock we passed half an hour ago.* Uncle Oscar said that the Needles were protected by an old Sheepeater Indian curse that was supposed to keep white men away. A small band of Sheepeaters tried to hide in the Needles when they were being rounded up by the cavalry in the 1800s. But the cavalry caught up with them and herded them to a reservation in Oklahoma, the ones that didn't starve to death or get killed. The curse didn't work back then, and it didn't keep hunters out now, just made it harder for them to find their way home.

My father took me up to the Needles just once, when I begged him so hard that Uncle Oscar said we could use his old red Jeep, the only thing that would make it up there.

"God, she's a strong willed kid," he scolded my father when he gave him the keys. But he grinned at me. "Don't let the evil spirits get you," he said, and when my eyes widened he laughed.

Uncle Oscar believed in such things. He planted wheat and dehorned and castrated cattle by the moon. Once Jake convinced him they couldn't wait for the new moon to castrate a herd of calves and the whole bunch almost bled to death. *There was blood all over the corral and we had to give every one of them antibiotics*, Oscar recalled proudly. *It almost broke us*. Of course he was exaggerating, but after that even my father was careful about when he dehorned cattle. "Oscar is just superstitious," I once heard Rose, a good Catholic, tell my mother. The old Finns were that way, she said, because they didn't get an education. She looked down on Oscar because he didn't even go to high school. But I had seen him around a spooked horse, how he could put his hand on its quivering flank and calm it right down, how he could look up in the clear blue sky and say it would rain and it would. I believed what he said about weather and the moon and the Needles.

We drove up an abandoned logging road that sometimes disappeared in the grass. The Willys bounced so hard in the deep ruts I had to hold on tight not to fall out. We wound up and up the mountainside for what seemed like hours, the trees and brush closing in so thick around the Jeep I couldn't see anything else.

"When will we get there?" I complained, straining to find the big black rocks that were so easy to see from the valley. "I know this is the right road," my father muttered, shifting down so the Jeep could make it up a particularly steep stretch. Suddenly we stopped. *There*, my father said, his eyes fixed on something behind me. I turned to look and nearly screamed: how had they kept hidden until now? A hundred yards away the Needles rose out of the timber and towered over us, impossibly huge, filling the horizon. I was close enough to see cracks as wide as a man in the sheer rocks, far enough away to see how the separate spires sprang from the ground with no warning, like the giant granite fingers of some horrible monster buried in the mountain beneath me. The tops of the Needles were so high I had to lean my head way back to see them.

"What do you think?" My father smiled, pleased that he could get us so close. I could only stare in silence. Then the sun disappeared behind a cloud and the wind came up suddenly, wooshing through the pine trees. It must have dislodged the rock that came bouncing down the steep slope toward us, big as a basketball and almost perfectly round. We jumped into the Jeep and watched the boulder roll right past us, crashing violently through the undergrowth, snapping thick branches like brittle bones. For a long time my father just looked at the place where it disappeared. "Let's go," he said.

Neither one of us spoke until we were out of their sight. *We made them mad,* I said, and he didn't laugh.

There were no craggy mountains close to our farm, just rolling foothills gathered at the base of Squaw Butte on the eastern horizon. Squaw Butte was a huge, oddly shaped landmass that looked amazingly like an Indian woman lying on her back looking up at the sky. The southern ridges of Squaw Butte were her hair and feather headdress flowing down, her legs and feet emerged in the north-running knolls. I couldn't look at Squaw Butte and not see the Indian. Some people said it was named for a massacre of Shoshoni women and children camped there for the winter, but I preferred the prettier story: that an early settler saw a beautiful Indian maiden in the mountain's profile. The sun rose right over Squaw Butte, silhouetting her face in blazing backlight. Squaw Butte was a magnificent Indian sleeping peacefully, snow-covered in winter, green in early spring, tawny brown all summer and fall.

The nearest real mountain was so far away from the farm that it shimmered in haze, a cone-shaped peak that stayed snowy all summer long. I didn't know its name, but I would climb up on the barn roof and stare at it for hours, imagining I was up there in a cool forest instead of sweltering in the valley heat. From the top of the barn I could see Squaw Butte in the middle distance and my mountain on the horizon beyond. I would take books up there to read, especially the ones I didn't want my parents to see. In third grade I found *The Aztec Conquerors* among my school's little library of mostly donated books. It was a heavy, thick volume, bound in blue with gold lettering. I casually pulled it from the shelf when I'd read practically everything else that looked promising, and realized immediately that it didn't belong in the "middle room" library for third, fourth, and fifth graders. The words were too big and the type was too small. I struggled to comprehend the long sentences and unfamiliar terms, and was about to give up when I got to the virgin sacrifice part.

The stale-smelling pages described, in gruesome detail, how the Aztecs would choose one of their most beautiful maidens, march her to the top of a huge temple, then cut out her heart and throw the bleeding sacrifice into a deep pit. The girls were selected like beauty queens, dressed in white of course, and made to walk up steep steps to a bloodstained altar. I read this part over and over and spent hours on the barn pretending to be an Aztec girl. Slowly, tragically, I would walk up the slanting roof, staring straight ahead, ready to meet my fate. The book contained a small drawing of what somebody imagined was an Aztec virgin sacrifice, and I held that image in my mind—the girl in the flowing white dress, the crowd of onlookers on the lower steps, the high priests in elaborate robes waiting at the top, the thick flat stone altar, like a bed or a table. Her sacrifice was made to ensure good fortune for the tribe. And then Cortes came.

I lost interest in the story then, even though it was still bloody enough. The Conquistador's predictable massacres, his merciless destruction of entire tribes, was not nearly as thrilling as one Indian priest carving out the heart of one willing victim. Cortes was driven by a crude greed for gold; there was no exquisite mystery in this. I had seen the dredge-despoiled Gold Fork in Long Valley. We passed abandoned dredge machines on our way to the ranch, rusting monsters with huge gears and pulleys and levers. They probably looked bigger in the scraped out river bed because there was nothing else there. Not a tree, not a bush, not a blade of grass. Dredging for gold—scooping up the ground, turning it upside down, and leaving it that way—made a moonscape in the middle of Long Valley, a barren stretch where not even lodgepole could grow in the gravelly offal. After the gold was gone these worthless hunks of metal lay mired in the tons of sand and muck they disgorged years ago, and Gold Fork ran black and shallow and dead through the middle of it all.

I pretended virgin sacrifice at the ranch too, on the dry treeless hill above the bunkhouse where real people were buried. I loved going to the homestead graveyard; it was scary of course, but so close to the ranch house I could almost see Rose through the big kitchen window. The wind blew all the time, swirling up dust around the headstones, muffling sounds from below. Inside the fence, it seemed we were floating above the rest of the world, the whole hilltop hovering on the moaning wind.

Nobody else I knew had their own family burial ground. This one was ringed in sagging barbed wire, a half-dozen monuments crumbling at the corners but still readable, garish pink plastic flowers on one of the graves. My grandparents, Hannah and Gustaf, were buried properly beneath a polished red granite headstone in the Long Valley Finnish Cemetery several miles away. That was a respectable resting place, kept green and park-like by the Finnish Ladies Aid Society, a hand-lettered sign over the entrance in Finnish and English asking visitors to please keep the grounds clean. The several hundred graves there were guarded by a white clapboard Finnish Lutheran Church that my grandfather helped to build. But the settlers who died before there was a church and a cemetery for Finns were buried right on their homesteads, not very deep, in pine boxes hewn by hand. It seemed that they were more likely to escape, and the thought thrilled me. From inside Rose's kitchen I could look up there and see the graveyard fence, the tops of the tilting headstones: *did something move?* It made me shiver sometimes, even sitting right next to the wood stove.

I knew a little about the ones buried there—Johan and Martta my great grandparents, my great aunt Helvie who died in childbirth, two or three tiny slabs of concrete for unnamed infants. Uncle Oscar pronounced the headstone names for me—*Yohawn. Marrrta* (rolling the r's—brrr!). Long wavy first syllables, stopping short on the second ones. I practiced saying them, sitting next to the graveyard fence, staring at each headstone and listening for a response. But there was only the incessant wind, or now and then a hawk screaming in the timber, or the door to the ranch house opening and slamming shut.

"Come on down now!" my father would call, waving his arms to get my attention. "We have to get back."

Going home, my parents might let me curl up in the back window of the car. The ranch, the Needles, Long Valley, and finally the forested canyon would disappear behind us, but I would try to hold onto it all, remembering how it felt to fly on the giant stride, or the leathery smell of Uncle Oscar's tack room lined with smooth saddles, or the glittering fool's gold and garnet-studded stones in Rose's rock garden. I would close my eyes and picture the graveyard, the tilting headstones and the flat concrete markers with just a year, 1898, or 1899, scrawled in the cement because the babies died right away without names. I would not think about going home, how hot and brown and boring it would be. And as the car swung gently around the canyon curves, descending in twilight, I would fall asleep.

Three

1957: ICHTHYOLOGY

FISH ARE IRRELEVANT TO IRRIGATION, at best an afterthought: *what shall we plant in the reservoir?* Fish are so easily ignored, invisible until you drain the creek to find them gasping on the bottom, mute unless they're sucked out of the stream. Pioneer farmers were crude flood irrigators. Just dam the creek and make a cut in the bank upstream; gravity does the rest. Never mind the babies poured out with the bathwater, acres of frantic trout suffocating in the muddy fields, flapping a final voiceless protest: *fish out of water.*

We came late to the extinction process, the last farms on canals channeled out of Black Canyon Reservoir, spared the dirty work of conquest. Of course there were no salmon in the Payette River, dammed decades before we arrived. Of course trout were rare below the dam, replaced by disgusting bony bottomfeeders: squawfish and suckers that didn't mind warm muddy water. Of course the best fishing was in irrigation ponds, stocked by farmers with a couple of buckets of bluegills and crappies and catfish taken from the reservoir or some other farmer's pond. I preferred catching bluegills because they fought back. There was no thrill in pulling up a catfish, inert as a tire, from the murky bottom.

Yet to a desert child all fish are exotic, worth a risk. I was glad to get even flat little bluegills and sluggish catfish, tempted with worms unearthed from a soggy ditchbank, my only tackle a hook, some lead sinkers, and a red-and-white plastic bobber. Pond fishing was primarily an exercise in patience, waiting, waiting for that bobber to go down. After a while, staring out at the rippling water, I could induce an hallucination: it was me bobbing on the wind-nipped waves, drifting to the opposite shore.

I could go by myself to Brown's Pond and bring home a bucket full of fish. Jack Brown had bulldozed the pond into being, scraping out a natural gully and pushing all the dirt into a high dam. The drain ditch running into the gully soon filled it up. Brown managed to hold enough water all year long to keep his fish alive. We had a pond, too, but it dried up in winter when the irrigation season was over. The year my father tried raising geese they practically lived in the pond, dropping huge goose poops to the bottom, foolishly staying there after dark when the coyotes came out. By late fall the pool had shrunk to a shallow puddle and finally there was no escape. We awoke to find the dirty water strewn with white feathers, evidence of the cunning of coyotes, the stupidity of domestic geese.

Brown's Pond was a weak solution of dissolved fertilizer and weedkillers, laced with cow pee and manure slime from the Holstein herds that trampled the shore, but his fish somehow survived. Bluegills, crappies, and catfish were finned equivalents of the fierce cats that thrived in our barns, the shepherd dogs that barked hysterically in our driveways. *Hard to kill.* You might drop a writhing cat off the barn roof into a cow trough, just to watch it splash in the water. You might decide your dog killed too many chickens and drive him across the river into the next county and dump him out. But the cats crawled out of the trough and streaked across the barnyard, their rough fur water-sleeked against their thin bodies, and were always around at milking time that same night, demanding to be fed. One morning weeks later that dumped dog would just show up in the yard, starved and limping but still alive, glad to be home.

Getting to Brown's Pond was easy. All I had to do was walk a half mile down the gravel county road, climb through a barbed wire fence, and tamp down a place to sit in the pasture grass along the edge, careful to avoid cowpies. Then it was just a matter of casting out far enough and waiting, remembering to watch out for the bull. I practiced casting in our driveway with my father's old Zebco reel and a sinker as big as my thumb. I would pick a place in the road where I wanted the sinker to land, drop the tip of the rod back over my shoulder, and try to release the line at just the right moment. If it was a good cast the reel made a raspy zing running out the line and dropped the sinker perfectly in the dust, raising a miniature cloud. But letting go too early or too late plopped the stupid lead clot at my feet, tangling my line into a terrible nest of knots, punishment for either eagerness or hesitation.

Bulls don't breathe; they snort. So I heard him before I saw him, standing just below me at the bottom of the grassy dam, tossing his head, snot dripping from the iron ring in his nose. I had been in one of my fishing trances, intent on the wind and water. Now I was absolutely focused on the bull, not twenty feet away, watching me. Holstein bulls were mean. Since she couldn't keep me home my mother filled me with stories of farmers pinned in corrals or gored against fences, of children trampled by bulls. We all knew how Tiny Martin, a huge, fat man, was killed by his bull right in the corral and in front of his wife, who could only stand rooted in the yard and scream.

I didn't move at first, imagining how far it was back to the fence, whether I could get there before he did. Running would only invite chase; it was best to walk. Slowly, carefully I let the fishing rod sink into the grass. I rose to my knees and stood up, never taking my eyes off the bull. One step back, then another, and another. He blinked, and shook his head, throwing off slobber and snot, but didn't move. Another step backward. Another. I glanced over my shoulder to gauge the distance to safety, and the bull bellowed. *Now!* Who wouldn't have laughed, watching me sprint across the pasture, ripping the back of my shirt on the barbed wire, not stopping until I was on the other side of the road and through another fence, into another field. Finally I dared to stop and look back. The bull was at the edge of the pond, investigating my fishing gear. He bent his big head down, snuffled the Zebco reel, then tentatively tasted the cork handle of my rod. I watched helplessly as he pushed over my bucket of live bluegills—fish I was catching for my own pond—and placed his heavy front hoof on the stainless steel pail. The metal buckled under his weight in an awful crackling collapse. At last he lumbered away from the ruined bucket, oblivious to my bluegills flopping desperately in the pasture grass. My father will kill me, I thought. But he just called Jack Brown and asked him to keep the bull out of the pasture while he went for the pole and bucket. I waited in the pickup. At least the fishing pole looked okay. When he came back to the truck and tossed the crumpled pail in the back I bit my lip, steeling for a scolding. Amazingly, he hugged me. *Next time I'll take you to Steiner's Pond,* he said, patting my back as if to comfort me, even though I wasn't crying.

Steiner's Pond was several miles away, a flooded gravel pit in the bottomlands of the Payette River behind the little town of Letha. It was much bigger and deeper than Brown's, with steep rocky banks. People said there were big fish in Steiner's Pond. You might hook a real monster.

I had seen pictures in our *World Book Encyclopedia* of monster catfish pulled from the Mississippi, too big to fit in a farmer's wagon. Of a gigantic sturgeon, taller than the man standing next to it, caught right in Idaho in the Snake River. That wasn't so far away. There might still be one left here.

A few days later at Steiner's Pond my father and I caught five bluegills, two crappies, and a big catfish to put in the new milk bucket. My father wore his leather work gloves to take the catfish off the hook. The sight of its squishy black body, its disgusting flat mouth and dripping whiskers, made me think of the monster in the *World Book*.

"I can throw it back," he offered, seeing me make a face. "No," I said. "I want him for my pond."

I was planning a fish pool, something I'd seen in a *Look Magazine* at my piano teacher's house. This pool was purely ornamental: an outlandish concept for a farm child. It was lined with rocks and filled with big orange goldfish. Lily pads floated on the clear surface. I would have to use pond fish and river rocks, but we had the perfect spot, under the big apricot tree behind our house, just a few feet from the ditch. My father could easily dig a hole in the soft ground. I would divert some ditchwater into the pool and plant it with whatever I could catch.

We finished the whole thing that same afternoon, his shovel pulling up pounds of mud with a violent sucking sound, me digging a shallow trench to the ditch. My river rocks wouldn't stick to the sides like it showed in the magazine picture, so I had to be satisfied with arranging them on the bottom. A good irrigator's daughter, I knew how to build a mud dam part way across the ditch and back water up into the trench. The ditchwater dutifully sought lower ground, finally splashing on the rocks at the bottom of my pond. I poured in the bucket of fish and waited. After a while the water cleared so I could see the bluegills and crappies darting among the rocks, the motionless dark catfish half buried on the bottom. I felt like a god.

The searing summer heat that grew our corn so fast sucked moisture right out of the ground. I had to turn water into my pond every day, or it would evaporate to nothing, even in the shade. Every morning I dammed the ditch and refilled the pool and dropped in some worms. It was entertainment enough until my father rented the house on our other place. That was what we called the farm adjoining ours: *the other place.* It had once belonged to a man named Murray, but my father bought him out, tore down the fences between our fields, turned our cattle into Murray's pastures, and used his barns and shops and corrals, obliterating the boundaries between us. Murray's forty acres, his barns and shop and empty house became extensions of ours. So when a young couple named Dave and Patty Johnson moved into the vacant house I felt crowded, exposed, as if they lived in my bedroom.

They were good renters until I ran them off. Patty kept the slanted linoleum floors shining, rubbed the windows with newspapers until they sparkled, even mowed the wild yard and planted flowers next to the step. Her new wifely enthusiasm fascinated me. I could stand in our yard and actually see her washing windows, sweeping the sidewalk, planting zinnias in their back yard. I could hear the screen door slam. She had been a majorette in high school; sometimes she would twirl a baton in the yard, passing it from hand to hand, flinging the silver shaft high into the air and catching it perfectly. Patty Johnson was irresistible.

It took me a couple of weeks to muster the courage to get closer. I waited until her husband left for his sawmill job in town, checked to make sure her pale blue Chevrolet was still in the driveway, and walked slowly to the house. The morning was already hot; their back door was open and I could see into the living room through the screen. I knocked louder than I meant to, banging the wooden screen door inside its frame. She appeared in the doorway immediately, showing her white teeth in a big friendly smile.

"Hi!" she said brightly, as if we already knew each other. She unlatched the screen door. "Come in and see my new batch of babies!"

She meant guppies. Patty Johnson kept two glass bowls for the tiny fish, one for the males and one for the pregnant females. The male guppies were smaller than minnows, but splashed with color, their iridescent sides flashing red and turquoise. The females were big and bland, at least twice the size of their mates. The pregnant ones looked a little like tadpoles before they grew legs. I stared, speechless, at one of the females giving birth. Baby guppies no bigger than an eyelash emerged from her bloated body and instinctively swam into the green plastic foliage floating in the bowl.

"They're hiding from the dads," Patty whispered. "That's why they're in a different bowl. The males eat the babies."

"I thought fish hatched from eggs," I said finally, my voice hoarse with amazement.

"Not these." Patty grinned. "They're special, don't you think?" She was obviously proud of her fish breeding operation. "When the babies get bigger, I can sell them back to the pet shop in Boise. Would you like some Kool-Aid?"

I tried to make polite conversation, sipping cherry Kool-Aid from a turquoise tin tumbler that gave my drink a slightly metal taste.

"I have a whole set," Patty said, holding up her yellow one for me to admire. "Eight different colors."

I nodded, uncertain about how to discuss tableware. We sat silent for a few moments. *I saw you twirling* I said finally, and her face brightened again.

"You did? Would you like me to show you?" She disappeared into the bedroom and emerged with the silver baton, spinning it idly in one hand, the big rubber end circling inside her slightly crooked arm, the smaller end on the outside. Her fingers moved magically on the shaft, her wrist twisting in and out with a rhythm as certain as my piano teacher's metronome. "Come outside—I'll teach you!" Patty pulled me up from the sofa so fast I almost spilled my red Kool-Aid.

Her baton was too long for my arms, so all I could do was watch her spin it back and forth, from hand to hand, behind her back, between her legs, and up into the air, catching it and laughing at me for ducking.

"If you come back tomorrow, I'll give you my first baton to practice with," she said. "I know it's around here somewhere."

I tried to learn twirling because it was a good excuse to see the guppies. We would practice for a while in her yard and then go inside for metallic Kool-Aid and to check the fish. How many new babies? Was this female ready to move to the birthing bowl? Should we put this one back with the males now? Like all farm children, I was casually familiar with animal husbandry, with the painful sounds of bulls breeding and cows calving and newborns emerging all covered with blood. But this miniature operation, with its barely perceptible acts of conception and birth, was much more interesting. I would squat in front of the fish bowls, my eyes inches from the glass, feeling huge and powerful and awkward. It was even worth bruising the inside of my arm purple with Patty's old baton. After a couple of weeks I could twirl it slowly, right-handed, but only if I really concentrated. *That's very good!* Patty would squeal, and I'd lose my place, jamming the end of the baton into my arm, making the painful bruise bloom even darker. I willed myself not to flinch.

Even after hours of practice I could not twirl the baton in my left hand. "That's okay," Patty grinned when I dropped it for about the hundredth time. "You can rest tomorrow. I'm taking some guppies to Boise."

I watched her leave the next morning, a dust cloud rising from the back of her Chevrolet as she disappeared up the road.

Her husband had already gone to work. From our yard I could see she left the back door open. The screen was locked, but I had a plan for getting in. I used one of my father's pencil-thin welding rods and only tore the screen a little bit forcing it through the mesh. The old-fashioned latch was nothing more than a nail with a fancy curve at one end, dropped into a heavy u-shaped staple in the door frame. I pushed the welding rod through the screen, moving it up and down to widen the hole a little, and angled it underneath the latch. When I pushed down on my end of the rod the latch flipped up easily. The whole thing took no more than a minute.

It was so quiet inside the house I could hear myself breathe, hear the padding of my dusty bare feet on the floor, practically hear the guppies swimming. Patty had a little net to catch them, and I brought a jar. I wanted just a male and a female—she had so many she would never miss two. A big female was easy to trap, but the males kept slithering out between the rim of the net and the side of the fishbowl. I splashed some water on Patty's shining linoleum. Finally I got a male in the net, but he flung himself sideways just as I was dropping him into the jar. He landed on the floor with a tiny splat. I crawled underneath the table, feeling along the baseboards until my fingers came upon something cold and wet and still. *Thank you God,* I sighed, but when I dropped the male in with my female, he floated to the top like a leaf. I thought for a moment, put the dead fish back in Patty's bowl, and caught another male, more careful this time to keep him in the net.

Outside the house, I used the welding rod to maneuver the latch back into place. Except for the hole in the screen, nothing was any different. Grasshoppers popped up out of the weeds as I walked the few hundred yards home, the cool glass pressed against my stomach under my T-shirt.

My mother was vacuuming so it was easy to slip into my room and hide the guppies. I sat on my closet floor and peered at them swimming inside the jar. "Do we have a glass bowl?" I asked when she shut off the roaring machine. "I caught some minnows in the ditch and I want something to put them in."

"I didn't know there were minnows out there," my mother said, but she got down a Pyrex mixing bowl and watched as I poured the guppies in. I put them on top of the television, where the light came in from a window and glinted on the male's iridescent sides. Maybe they'll have babies too, I thought, imagining the water thick with little fish.

It was almost dark when Patty got home. Her husband drove in later. From my parents' bedroom window, I watched their lights come on. The house seemed far away somehow. I put Patty's baton under my bed. I would never go back there.

How do parents feel when their child grudgingly admits she is a thief? How did I feel, trudging through the dust after dark between them, holding the bowl of guppies next to my body, careful not to let the water splash out? Patty opened the door and looked down at me with the guppies in the Pyrex bowl and for once she wasn't smiling. *I took these*, I whispered. She only nodded.

"We're awful sorry," my father said, his voice pleading. "It won't happen again."

He looked at the hole in the screen; it seemed much bigger now.

"I'll fix the door, too."

The Johnsons moved to town a few weeks later. Patty was going to have a baby, my mother said, and she wanted to be closer to the doctor. We didn't talk again, but late one night before Patty left I sneaked up to their door, laid her baton on the step, and ran back as fast as I dared in the dark. Shimmering stars floated overhead and the warm night air caressed my face, like water.

The summer grew stifling, pushing the red line in my father's shop thermometer past the 100-degree mark every day. Finally he agreed to take us to the ranch. I was elated. Now that I couldn't visit Patty there was nothing to do. My fish pond seemed crude and ugly, and I only went out there because I had to refill it every morning. I longed to escape the boredom and guilt, to wake up in a different bedroom, Aunt Rose's sheets cold and crisp against my skin. I would fling myself into the air on the giant stride or ride Sandy, Oscar's gentlest horse, up into the timber and just forget everything.

We would even go fishing in Cascade Lake. It was really just a reservoir, a huge shallow pool along the west side of Long Valley. People called it a lake, Uncle Oscar said, to make the land around it cost more. He snorted in disgust. Those ranches underneath the reservoir were practically stolen, he said, and now the damn real estate developers are selling lots on the shoreline for more than Henry Maki got for his whole place, buildings and all. But you could drive right up to where the old highway disappeared underwater, and fish from the road. One afternoon my father took me there and we cast into water that covered homestead cabins and barns and even a little town, Arling, abandoned when the government came in and condemned the land for the reservoir. I stood next to the car, squinting to see my bobber and trying to imagine the submerged houses, fish swimming in and out the doors and windows, when something took my hook so hard it nearly pulled the pole from my hands.

"You've got one sis!" My father grinned as I furiously tried to reel in, but the fish was so strong he pulled the line out even farther, the reel zinging backwards. My father stood behind me while I fought the fish. "Bring him in slow," he cautioned. "Don't jerk the pole, you might lose him." It was all I could do to turn the reel, inch by inch, dragging my monster to shore. Finally I was pulling him through the shallow water, his long dark body half revealed, astounding in size. I walked backwards, dragging the fish up into the grass. He flopped a few times and lay still.

"What is it?" I shrieked. "A sturgeon? A trout?" My father knelt to inspect it, then turned to me, disappointed.

"It's a sucker," he said. "Biggest damn one I've ever seen." I dropped the pole and moved closer to my catch: a horrible huge trash fish, its disgusting round mouth made for bottom feeding, its ugly dark body stuffed with whatever it strained from the mud. The creature flopped suddenly, startling me.

"Kill it!" I screamed. "It's awful!" My father picked up a big rock to smash in its head and I ran crying back to the car. That night at dinner Oscar said the suckers and squawfish were taking over the reservoir, you couldn't hardly catch a trout anymore. Maybe the Fish and Game would plant some rainbows in there.

We drove home the next day, dropping down the river canyon from a cool mountain morning to a blazing desert afternoon. "I've got to get water on that corn tonight," my father said as he pulled into the dusty driveway. "Everything's dried up." Suddenly I remembered my pond. I jumped out of the car and ran through the yard to the apricot tree. My fish were on their sides, flapping in a few inches of water, but still alive. Without thinking I scooped them up and threw them in the irrigation ditch. If the catfish stung me I didn't feel it. My bluegills and crappies and even the catfish darted away down the ditch. I realized then I could have saved them just by turning water into the pool, but the fish were free now, feeling the pull of moving water for the first time. If they were lucky they might make it to a drain ditch, and from there maybe even find the river.

Four

1958: Transients

PATTY JOHNSON AND HER HUSBAND moved out in one day, their last pickup load bouncing up our rutted road just at dusk. I couldn't wait until morning to go over there, even though it meant being alone in the darkening house. This time the doors were flung open, a final mocking message: no need to break in anymore.

I walked slowly through the silent rooms, my dusty bare feet leaving tracks on Patty's once-gleaming floors. In the living room, this space was where her couch had been, with a low coffee table in front for our Kool-Aid glasses. Against that wall was where Patty put the stand for the fishbowls. In the next room her bed had been covered with a white chenille bedspread. I remembered how the soft nubby fabric felt against the backs of my bare legs as I watched Patty rummage in the closet, searching for her high school majorette uniform. The closet had been stuffed with clothes and boxes; now it was so empty I could stand inside and breathe Patty's smell, her Jergens hand lotion and Rayette hair spray and Evening in Paris cologne, all mixed in with her husband's Jade East aftershave. On one wall she had hung their wedding picture, his family lined up on one side, hers on the other, everybody smiling. Just a nail hole left.

For the first time I sensed the impermanence of people's lives. I had lived in the same house since before I could remember, had the same rural route box, the same phone number, the same piano, couch, kitchen table. We rarely even moved the furniture. The walls had absorbed our family smells of cooking and detergent and floor wax, my dad's sweat and cigarette smoke, the slightly sour bathroom odor. I could walk through those rooms with my eyes closed and never run into anything. I could find the light switches in the dark, could reach for the phone without looking, knew what was in every cupboard, every drawer. This knowledge was a source of boredom and comfort.

Now in the silence of that vacant house I realized we could be gone too, leaving behind only some strange lingering smells and the dents in the floor where the furniture had been, the chips in the sink where I had once dropped a brown glass Purex bottle, the scars on the kitchen linoleum from the day I roller-skated in-

side, the outlines of our picture frames on the empty walls. Nobody would know that this is where I always sat on the floor and watched television, *I Love Lucy* in the mornings, *The Wonderful World of Disney* and *Ed Sullivan* on Sunday nights, *The Little Rascals* right after school. That this corner was where we put the Christmas tree. That this window was where I stood watching for my father to come in from elk hunting in the fall, after he had been gone for two weeks or more, where I

Christmas at the Emmett farmhouse, 1956

stood waiting to see his truck headlights turn down our driveway, coming home. Nobody would know. These thoughts made me feel light headed, weightless, almost sick. I rushed outside and let the damaged screen door slam behind me. Nobody would know that I made those holes in the screen, or why. Even crime scenes become meaningless.

I sat on the steps and watched the lights come on in our house, heard our swamp cooler buzzing in my parents' bedroom window, the faint sounds of some television program drifting out the open living room door. Our house suddenly seemed small and fragile, our dull routines, amazing.

We didn't rent the other place for almost a year. It was a miracle that Barbara Jean's family found us. My father didn't advertise it in the paper, but that wouldn't have done them any good anyway. Barbara Jean said they just heard about it somewhere, the same way they heard that there was work in the Idaho sawmills and drove clear from Tennessee though not one of them, not Barbara Jean's big flat-footed mother or her scrawny little father or least of all her mother's crazy brother, could read a word. All they knew was to stay on the road with the US 40 sign, heading west. Barbara Jean was proud of the fact they came all that way without a map, just taking number 40 and heading toward the sunset and into Idaho on number 55, getting to Emmett, and then finding the right county roads out to our farm. What else could my father say to these strangers with everything they owned in a rickety truck, the crazy brother riding in the back, but yes, he would let them have the house for forty dollars a month.

Barbara Jean was eight, just a year younger than me, but she had never been to school since her little sister Shirley was too young and her mother said they had to go together. Barbara Jean was skinny and freckled with straight white-blond hair snipped off just below her ears. Shirley was dark like the father with curls down her back. She trailed Barbara Jean like a shadow. Shirley did not speak but Barbara Jean did her talking. *Shirley would like a drink, do y'all got any soda pop? Shirley needs to pee, where's the bathroom?* Shirley was five years old now so soon Barbara Jean could go to school. They had a baby brother named Junior who seemed glued to his mother's broad hip, a bottle always stuck in his mouth. I loved the way Barbara Jean said y'all and ran her words together like musical notes and told me things I had never heard of before, like how much good stuff you could find that people just threw away. I went once with Barbara Jean and Shirley and their mother and father to the county dump and found a perfectly good yellow circle skirt that stood straight out from my waist when I twirled around. *See what I told you,* Barbara Jean said, grinning. *Ain't it perty?*

My mother forbade me to go to the dump with them ever again but she could not keep me from walking over to the other place to play with Barbara Jean and Shirley in what remained of our summer. I would knock on their door and the mother would wordlessly let me in or let Barbara Jean and Shirley out. I showed them how to catch barn cats and drop them off the loafing shed roof into the watering trough, how to play pioneers in the old wagons on the high dry hill in the pasture, even let them try my hoola-hoop. Barbara Jean could keep it going longer than anyone, holding her hands above her head and whooping with delight. Sometimes I would catch a glimpse of her mother's brother, sneaking around the corner of the house, looking over his shoulder, always grinning. Once her mother let him play a trick on us. She told us to go down in the cellar and get some potatoes. Just when we were all on the bottom step in the dank-smelling dark he jumped out, waving his arms and growling like a mean dog. Barbara Jean grabbed my hand and Shirley's hand and we stood there screaming until the mother came down. By this time Shirley was so scared she was bawling and hiding her head in Barbara Jean's side. The mother laughed at us and said *y'all are a bunch of fraidy cats,* but she wouldn't let her brother follow us up out of the cellar.

Barbara Jean's family lived a much more exciting life than mine. All they had to eat for six days out of the week was buttermilk and white bread, worse fare even than the fried hamburger and stringy macaroni and cheese my mother cooked. But on Friday nights they ate delicacies I rarely tasted—potato chips and crunchy pork rinds and hot dogs and ice cream and soda pop for the kids and beer for the grownups. They gave Junior beer in his bottle and he drank it all down. The dad would turn up their radio loud on KGEM, the country music station, and do some strange stomping dance to the fast songs, whooping and gulping down beer and just tossing the empty bottles on the floor, where they rolled around under our feet. The crazy uncle drank and danced too, taking Barbara Jean and Shirley by the hand and twirling them so fast they fell down. Barbara Jean's mother seemed happiest during these little parties, smiling shyly when her scrawny little husband grabbed onto her and pulled her around the room, his heavy boots just missing her big bare feet. I gaped at this spectacle like a missionary among savages. I had never seen adults behave this way.

Barbara Jean and I danced too in the afternoons, when *American Bandstand* came on television. Every day at 4 o'clock the familiar *Bandstand* music would play and Dick Clark would grin into the camera and the kids in the background would cheer. Sometimes he would shout "Hello, all you folks out there in Boise, Idaho!" like he was trying to make contact with a distant planet. He pronounced it "Boy-zee," the same way John Cameron Swayze said "Oregone," or "Nevahdah" if he was talking about the bomb tests. I could tell Dick Clark meant his greeting as a joke, that to him back in Philadelphia, Boise was a hick place in the middle of nowhere. But Boise was the biggest city in my world.

We taught ourselves the newest dance, the twist. I would wear the yellow circle skirt and spin around until it flared almost to my waist. Sometimes my mother even joined in. The trick, she said, was to put one foot out and pretend to smash a cigarette with your toe while you dried your bottom with an imaginary towel, one end of it in either hand. We twisted until our sides ached and then flopped on the floor to watch the gyrating *Bandstand* girls in their bouffant hairdos and tight skirts. My favorite was Carmen, with her black mascaraed eyes and a strange white streak in her dark hair. She looked exotic and knowing, possessed of a secret to happiness that I would never learn. I loved watching her dance close with a cute boy to some slow song, "Put Your Head on My Shoulder" or "Angel Baby." *It's just like heaven being here with you. You're like an angel, too good to be true.* The kids on *American Bandstand* were always smiling, their hair was always perfect, their clothes the latest styles. Barbara Jean and I watched all this in our little living room, with its worn sofa and scuffed floor and the harsh summer sun streaming in through the windows, acres of Idaho farmland stretching out in every direction, as unimaginable to Carmen as Mars.

One day after *Bandstand* Barbara Jean picked out a Childcraft book and asked me to read it to her and Shirley. The Childcrafts came free when my mother bought a set of *World Book Encyclopedias*, and I had already read the good ones, *Poems of Early Childhood, Folk and Fairy Tales, Stories of Other Lands.* Barbara handed me *Poems.*

We ain't got many books at our house, she said. We sat on the couch, Barbara Jean on one side of me and Shirley on the other, her fat little legs sticking out straight, her bare feet black with dirt. I read "Old Mother Hubbard," "Over in the Meadow," and "This is the House that Jack Built." It felt strange, as if I were suddenly much older than they were. Barbara Jean stared at the words on the page while Shirley pointed to the pictures and giggled.

"More!" Shirley cried when I stopped, the first word she ever said to me. I was turning the pages to find "Wynken, Blynken and Nod" when Barbara Jean stood up suddenly and grabbed Shirley's hand.

We got to go, she said, pulling Shirley to her feet. I followed them home, our bare feet patting deep prints in the soft dust. Barbara Jean was strangely quiet. *How long you been able to do that?* she finally asked. She meant read.

I shrugged. "I don't know, since before I went to school I guess."

"Next year I'm goin' to school," Barbara Jean said. "Me and Shirley both!" She said it like I might disagree.

"Oh, you'll like our school," I said quickly. "It's got swings and a merry-go-round and cement to roller-skate on."

Barbara Jean shook her head, drawing circles in the dust with her toe. "We won't be here," she said softly.

In September Barbara Jean's daddy lost his job and they packed up their truck and left owing rent. Barbara Jean said they were going to a sawmill somewhere in Oregon. "I'll send y'all the rent money," her daddy said to my father before they drove away in the loaded truck. My father barely nodded. Barbara Jean was in the front seat, wedged between her mother and Shirley. She wouldn't look up.

"That's the last time I rent to Okies," my father said, spitting in disgust as the creaking truck pulled away. Barbara Jean's crazy uncle waved to us but I didn't wave back.

"I bet they left that house in a mess," my father said. "Let's go take a look."

I shook my head. "It's just empty again," I said. "Nothing to see."

Five

1959: BALANCE OF TERROR

M Y FATHER DID NOT FIGHT in the world war. This was a source of shame and power for my mother, whose brothers all went. Uncle Roy was in the army and Charles and George were sailors. My father got out on some kind of deferment, because he was a farmer or had flat feet or something. It was too important to talk about. My father never mentioned it except to defend himself against my mother's ridicule. He did this poorly, mumbling, his head down. Obviously she was right: he was afraid.

Other fathers fought. In first grade Larry Thompson and Glen Hadley brought their dads' black-bound war books to school and showed them to us during noon recess. The narrow volumes looked like high school annuals, but they were full of pictures of dead bodies and grinning GIs: crude, honest snapshots, like you might take of your family at a picnic. I wolfed down my fried egg sandwich and raced behind the building to find a hushed group already huddled around Glen and Larry. We gaped at the grainy photographs of Japanese corpses lined up on the ground, American soldiers squatting behind them, cradling their rifles. Close-ups of bullet holes in a head, the slanted eyes still open, blood oozing down the face. A body dangling on a barbed-wire fence, entrails spilling out. Charred corpses burned up, Glen said, in the underground caves where the enemy hid.

I stared at the pictures and could almost smell the mud and gore and singed hair. We were farm children and knew first hand of slaughter, of chopping heads off chickens, of butchering hogs, of slabs of meat hanging in the barn, hooves still attached. We barely noticed the spurting blood when our fathers dehorned cattle. We understood that one moment a pheasant was flying frantically away from the hunters and the next it was a warm lump of feathers on the ground. That night at dinner we knew to be careful chewing on the sinewy meat: you might break a tooth on buried buckshot. Still the war book pictures nauseated me. This was no cowboy show shoot-out, where Gene or Roy picked off a bad guy who died neatly and at a distance. This was not even like the war movies on TV, where death was a punishment for the enemy or an honor for us. I was shocked to realize that some of the corpses in the photographs were Americans. You had to look close to see the difference between the bloated bodies. My stomach lurched suddenly and I turned away, squeezing my eyes shut and gulping in air.

"Look at the scaredy cat!" Glen hooted derisively. "She's gonna puke!"

"I am not!" I shouted, but I kept my eyes closed. It didn't matter. I had looked so hard that the rotting bodies floated in reverse image on the inside of my eyelids—my memories now.

Uncle Roy was the only one of my relatives I ever heard really talk about the war, but he didn't know I was listening. He was drinking coffee with my mother in the kitchen; I was straining to hear from the living room, pretending to read a book. Uncle Roy had been in France. They were in this little town, he said, no bigger than Emmett, with narrow cobblestone streets and a big church. The Americans set a 6 o'clock curfew; after that nobody was supposed to be outside. They had to do this because the Germans could come back. Uncle Roy sat in the church tower with some other soldiers and watched for them. One night, long after six, this old woman came running down the street toward the church. Her white hair was streaming out behind her. The soldiers yelled for her to stop, to get back in her house, but she just kept running.

"We had to shoot her, sis," Uncle Roy said. "I don't know which one of us did, but we had to, you understand?" Then he started to sob. I held my breath, terrified now they might discover me. "I still dream about it," he choked. "Except in the dream it's our mother. *Our mother,* Jean!" My mother murmured something and pushed back her chair. She was walking towards me. I scrunched down and pulled the book so close to my face that the words blurred together. Her footsteps stopped in the doorway and I could feel her angry gaze.

"Get in your room!" she hissed. "This is none of your business!"

I flopped on my bed and stared up at the ceiling, imagining the white-haired woman in the street. I could not put my grandmother's face on her, because I did not remember my grandmother, even though she had lived at our house in the months before she died. Then she went to stay with Aunt Audrey, my mother's sister, and one day Aunt Audrey called on the phone from Boise and my mother started to cry—a terrible and terrifying wail. My mother ran into her bedroom and shut the door and my father took me on his lap. "Your grandmother"—he began hoarsely, and stopped, searching for the right words. "She died," I said matter-of-factly. Of course. How could it be anything else, anything less?

None of us cousins could attend the funeral because we were too young to understand. Audrey's daughter Pat was the oldest, just turned six, and she begged her mother to at least let her go. I was only four and glad to be excused from something that sounded just like church except with a coffin in the room. Plus it was unnerving to see so many adults sobbing and hugging each other. Even my father wiped away tears and blew his nose when he drove Pat and me to Uncle Roy's house, where his wife Delores would watch us. *I wish they'd stop crying* I confided to Pat as we sat scrunched up in the back seat of our car, wedged between funeral wreaths. Her face flushed and she glared at me.

"They're sad—we're all sad about it but you!" She was practically shouting. "Don't you see? Grandma's gone! She's never coming back!"

And then she started bawling. My father glared at me in the rear view mirror. I pretended to study the flower arrangement pressed against my shoulder—huge red gladiolus, their celery stalks stuck in a horseshoe-shaped wire mesh and "Good-bye" written in gilt on a ribbon holding the whole thing together. It had little spikes coming out the bottom, to push in the ground at the cemetery. *Don't you make Patty cry*, my father warned, and his stern voice somehow comforted me. Pat was wrong. I knew our grandmother was dead, and I knew she wasn't coming back, just the same as a dog hit by a car and lying in the barrow pit was not going to get up again. But I felt no connection between her death and my life, any more than I could imagine myself cold and stiff by the side of the road.

The author, her cousin, grandmother, and uncle in front of the Emmett farmhouse, 1955

Until I was nine war happened only in history and death was a singular event, taking first my grandmother and then a great uncle or aunt I'd never met, or Tiny Martin gored by his bull or famous people on the news, Buddy Holly who sang Peggy Sue on American Bandstand crashing in a plane or James Dean wrecking his car. These were manageable, imaginable. I realized, hypothetically, that my parents would die someday, but resolved simply to kill myself just before that happened so I wouldn't have to be without them. Of course this was an absurd plan—I never considered how I would know when they were about to die or what I might do if they didn't go together—but it was enough to hold off terror for a while. Mostly I was distracted from mortality by school and summer vacations and Christmases and secret crushes and riding horses and swimming in the canal, and more and more, by television: Lucy and Ricky, Spanky and Alfalfa, Wally and the Beaver populated my empty world, connected me to a happier life. I watched Roy Rogers and Gene Autry and *The Cisco Kid* and *Sky King*. I saw Elvis Presley for the first time on the *Ed Sullivan Show*. I even watched the news. I saw Edward R. Murrow and a show about migrant workers and a girl my age who worked in the fields and never got to go to school. I watched Jackie Gleason and *Your Hit Parade* and *What's My Line* and then I discovered *Playhouse 90*.

Playhouse 90 came on late at night and was different from other TV shows. There were no cheerful brightly lit sets like on *Lawrence Welk*, no laugh tracks like behind *The Honeymooners—one of these days, Alice, pow!*—no unseen audience erupting hysterically. *Playhouse 90* was dark and so quiet you could hear the actors breathing. There was nothing between you and the actors on the shadowy stage, and after a while they seemed more like real people than Ozzie and Harriet Nelson or even the smiling Lennon Sisters. The people on *Playhouse 90* talked to each other, not to the camera. There were very few commercials to take your mind off their problems. When they argued it made you uncomfortable, like watching your parents fight. When they kissed you turned away, embarrassed. *Playhouse 90* was more like Glen and Larry's war books: it repelled and attracted me at the same time.

The last time I watched *Playhouse 90* it showed *Alas, Babylon*, a play about World War III. This was 1959 and by now we knew all about the bomb. Every week or so it was on the news that the army made another test explosion in Nevada—the newscasters from New York called it "Nev-ah-dah." We were doing this to scare the Russians off from starting another war. I had seen the billowing mushroom clouds on television and in our Civil Defense films at school. Sometimes after an atomic test, rain would fall in milky drops on our house and our fields, ruining my mother's clean windows.

"It's the bomb again," my father would announce when he saw whitish rivulets running down the ruts in our driveway. He noticed that this rain left a grey film on his pasture grass and haystacks, but it didn't seem to hurt the cows. The bomb infuriated my mother. She was especially proud of her gleaming windows, even if the house was dirty inside. As soon as the storm stopped she would be out there, rubbing chalky smears off the glass.

The year I was in second grade the newspaper reported thirty-two successful hydrogen bomb tests at the Nevada Proving Grounds. The bombs were called "devices." Decades later the government would release a study on fallout from the Nevada tests. It said that the county where we lived had been the "hottest" in Idaho, precisely the wrong place to be when the wind blew in from the south, pushing cold-war clouds.

One morning right after a bomb rain two Civil Defense men came to our school with a Geiger counter. None of us had ever seen a real one before, and we stared at it like it might explode. The Geiger counter was a black metal box with gauges and dials and a hose snaking out that one man held like a welding wand.

"Now there's nothing to be afraid of!" our teacher Mrs. Bradshaw beamed as the man waved the Geiger counter wand back and forth over our desks and our books and even down our arms and legs. I heard a faint crackle when he passed the wand across my shoes. "Does that mean I'm radioactive?" I asked. I had heard that word on the news. He smiled. *Nothing serious,* he said. But the other man, the one writing things down in a notebook, made a disapproving grunt and looked right at me then just for a second. He shook his head, ever so slightly. No one else saw this contradiction, and it made me shiver. Until that moment Civil Defense had been reassuring, even boring. Our teacher had showed us their cheerful cartoon about the little turtle, so we knew what to do if the Russians sent over a bomb and we didn't have time to get home: duck and cover. I felt silly crouching under my desk, but soon Mrs. Bradshaw would clap her hands and we could stand up. "Very good boys and girls!" she'd say, smiling broadly. "You did that in just ten seconds and so orderly too!" Fire drills were more fun; at least we got to go outside.

The two Civil Defense men left during noon recess, when I was sitting on the front steps putting on my roller skates. The smiling one came out first and put the Geiger counter in the trunk of their big grey car. He got in on the driver's side. I didn't pay much attention because I couldn't get the toe tight enough on one skate—it fell off my shoe every time I tried to stand. "Damn!" I muttered, angrily kicking the useless skate against the concrete step. My precious recess minutes were ticking away. *Let me help you*, a voice behind me said, and I turned to see the other man, the one with the notebook. Wordlessly I handed him my skate key. He knelt on the cement, just like my father might, and gently positioned my foot back in the skate. His big hand turned the key easily until it pinched into my shoe.

"There," he said, "try it now." I waved my foot in the air, trying to dislodge the skate, but it was on tight. When I stood up, wobbling unsteadily on the pitted cement, he took hold of my arm. "Don't fall now," he said, smiling right at me as he slipped the skate key into my jacket pocket. I started to move away but he held on.

"Do you drink milk?" he asked.

I shook my head without thinking about this strange question.

"Ugh, I hate it!" I said defiantly, expecting the usual adult disapproval. Instead he laughed. *Good girl*, he whispered, like it was a secret between us, and then the driver in the grey car honked the horn and he let go of my arm. I darted onto the concrete slab, merging into a stream of skating girls. When I put my hand in my pocket, the metal skate key was still warm from his touch.

I remembered his question years later, when the doctor in *Alas, Babylon* explained how cow's milk got contaminated. The doctor was one of the few people still alive in Florida after the Russians launched their missiles at us. I learned a new vocabulary watching *Playhouse 90* that night—SAC, ICBM, NORAD, DEW Line, Conelrad, fireball, flash burn, Strontium 90.

The play's hero, Randy, knew a war was coming because his brother in the Strategic Air Command sent him a telegram signed "Alas, Babylon," their code warning. Randy bought a lot of groceries and whiskey to get ready. Then all he could do was wait. I saw only what he would see of the nuclear war: when a warhead exploded there was a distant rumble and flash of light in his windows. The floors shook. A terrified bird fell on the porch. I watched helplessly as the characters tried to survive without gasoline, medicine, running water, electricity. Randy bought a hundred pounds of meat to keep in the freezer when he knew the war was coming. It was a white chest freezer just like the one we had in our garage. One day Randy smelled something and opened the freezer to find packages of rotting meat floating in warm water. He gagged.

Randy had a map of the United States on his wall, and finally he got a broadcast on his transistor radio from the President, a woman in the government who happened not to be in Washington when the Russians bombed it. The real President and Vice-President and all the others next in line were dead. This woman President was explaining what was left of the country. Denver was the capital now because Washington, D.C., was gone. Almost all our big cities were destroyed, but other places were hit too, because they were close to military bases. As she talked Randy used a black marker to cross out big areas on his map. I held my breath when the woman President started to talk about the western United States. Surely we would be okay—there was nothing to bomb out here! But I had forgotten about all the military bases and atomic reactors in the empty West. Mountain Home Air Force Base was not far away, and there were others in Washington, Montana, Wyoming, Utah, Nevada—a ring of targets around my home. The woman President calmly announced the destruction of cities I had actually been to: Salt Lake, Spokane, Portland, Seattle. Randy made a big X across the entire Northwest.

Alas, Babylon ended with the sound of a helicopter landing, bringing in men with Geiger counters just like the one I had seen at school. Randy asked who won the war. "We did," one of the men said. "Not that it really matters." And then the screen darkened and it was over. For a long time I sat on the floor in front of the TV, filled with a strange new fear. Or maybe it was the breaking loose of a fear that had been building every time we had a duck-and-cover drill, every time it rained bomb dust, every time a newscaster announced another successful test or talked about the Russians and the cold war or showed pictures of their May Day parade with the rows and rows of missiles rolling down the street. For the first time I understood that a nuclear war could really happen, that it would kill me and everyone I knew, and be horrible beyond imagining.

That night I dreamed about my grandmother. She was alive, and wearing a flowery dress, and all the cousins were running toward her, calling *Grandma! Grandma!* She smiled and held out her arms to us and we were hugging her and trying to climb on her lap when pieces of her flesh came off in our clamoring hands. The meat slipped off her bones in bloody slabs, wrinkled skin and all. We fell back in terror, screaming, trying to get away. I was running in that terrible slow motion way, hardly moving, and crying out *no no no no* when my mother shook me awake. "It's a nightmare," she said, "just a dream."

After she left I waited for a long time in the darkness and then tiptoed into my brother's room and got into his bed, careful not to touch him. He would be furious if I woke him up. But it was the only way I could get back to sleep.

For a long time afterwards I could not watch television at all. It seemed that every show was about some kind of danger. I was terrified of the dark, afraid to go to sleep. My brother made fun of me and warned me not to get into bed with him ever again but sometimes I had to. Night after night I woke up screaming, sometimes about being caught in a nuclear war, sometimes about a murderer in my room, sometimes about falling, falling from a very high cliff. I was ten years old and suddenly I was afraid to be away from my mother. I clung to her in the grocery store, convinced that if we got separated I might lose her forever. The Cuban Missile Crisis in sixth grade only made it worse. Our teacher Mr. Canfield brought his radio to school that day so we could hear it all, and when the announcer shouted "they're turning back!" Mr. Canfield, usually a stern, expressionless man, applauded wildly. "We sure showed them!" he crowed, but I was not relieved.

Then the strangest thing of all began to happen. I could be anywhere—just sitting in school, or eating supper in the kitchen, or riding my horse—and for no reason everything around me and inside me would speed up, like a 45 rpm record set on 78, and get louder and louder in my head. I became acutely aware of my slightest motion, of my breathing and my heartbeat, all going faster and faster. I was afraid I would explode. I learned that if I closed my eyes and breathed very slowly I could bring things back to normal, but I never told anyone. How could I even describe it? With my bomb nightmares, and my ridiculous fear that my mother would leave me every time she was out of my sight, people would think I was crazy.

The author, Easter Sunday, 1958

Six

1960: Last Suppers

THE WORD SURGED OUT of Salt Lake City and roared north, irreversible as the mighty Bonneville Flood fifteen thousand years before. That prehistoric torrent burst from Lake Bonneville and thundered through what would be Idaho, carving new canyons in the desert floor, littering the landscape with spectacular sediment. It was a deluge worthy of God himself, draining a lake that had covered most of modern Utah, just a briny puddle left behind. Brigham Young's followers gasped when he pointed to the salt-choked sea and proclaimed *this is the place*, but he was right. The Mormon pioneers dammed innocent creeks flowing down from the Wasatch Mountains and metered water to their farms, making the desert bloom. Soon the Saints overflowed even the vast Bonneville lakebed and moved out, armed with shovels and scripture, inflicting the promised land with their miraculous technology of dams and canals and ditches. Irrigation as religion, and as sacrilege.

As a child I knew nothing of this history. My only clue to the Bonneville Flood was a highway billboard that tried to make a joke of the big round rocks the floodwaters had deposited in the Idaho desert. "Petrified watermelons," the sign announced. "Take one home to your mother-in-law." I was ignorant of the Mormons until I started school.

My mother was a Christian Scientist, a religion so rare in our isolated farming community it provoked more curiosity than disapproval. Christian Science was created by a woman, Mary Baker Eddy, who said you could cure a sickness or heal a wound by refusing to believe in it. Our neighbors imagined Christian

Scientists as an odd but benign New England cult, in a category with the Quakers. The name itself was puzzling. Science, except when it increased bushels per acre or milk production, was the enemy of Christianity.

My father had been Finnish Lutheran, forced to endure Sunday worship in the little white church his father and some other immigrant Finns built next to their cemetery in the Idaho mountains. For twenty years he prayed and sang with the other *Suomalainens*, but his faith faded when he left the cold high country settlement for an irrigated rowcrop farm on the edge of a desert. The church was just old Finlander tradition that didn't fit anymore. He forgot his musical language, anglicized his foreign last name, abandoned blood bread and sauna baths. Soon most of the old Finns had moved on to the cemetery. The only services in the church were their funerals.

I was four and my brother still a baby when my mother took us to town to be baptized. I barely remember a silver bowl on a starched white cloth, the cold water sprinkled on my forehead, my brother wailing, the minister's murmurs. I knew this was supposed to mean something: the grownups were taking it very seriously. My mother stood stiff and solemn, Steve squirming in her arms. She stared straight ahead through the prickly netting of her little black hat, grim but determined. After that we made an obligatory appearance in church on Easter Sundays, a genuflection which fooled nobody. My mother could not embrace the Presbyterians' heartless Calvinism, but our baptism was a necessary defensive action, an attempt to save us from the Mormons.

They outnumbered us by far and recognized no differences between our various non-Mormon faiths. In their world, there were two camps: Saints and gentiles. This made for a certain religious tolerance among the protestants. Lutherans, Episcopals, Presbyterians, even Baptists were willing to ignore their doctrinal differences, were actually grateful for the small Catholic parish with its statue of Mary on the lawn. They recognized the true theological threat, ready to roll over us all.

For every one of our non-Mormon congregations there were half a dozen LDS "wards" whose members shared the same church building. Mormon churches were all built of smooth maroon brick and topped with a tall spire. You could always spot one, even before you saw the scrolly sign announcing *The Church of Jesus Christ of Latter Day Saints*. The sameness of the church buildings, right down to the lettering on their signs, was dictated from Salt Lake. These were monuments to absolute conformity, hard proof of a monolithic power emanating from Utah. Just seeing a Mormon church could make a gentile shiver.

But I was Presbyterian in only the most perfunctory sense; my mother really followed the crazy teachings of a Boston bluestocking with three names. I was no Lutheran; my father had long fallen away from his family's immigrant church. I had no opposing dogma to deflect the relentless proselytizing of my Mormon schoolmates, missionaries all. They knew I was the perfect target, unprotected and eager to fit in.

In first grade Dale Hansen calmly informed me that because I wasn't Mormon I would go to hell. The Hansens were rich—a fact that set them apart from most other Mormons, with their multitudes of children and dutiful church tithes eating up the money. Mr. Hansen was a Mormon stake president, even more important than a bishop, and their family lived in a new brick home, not our typical ramshackle farmhouse with its added-on rooms. The Hansen children dressed well by our standards and spoke impeccable English. They said "ahv" for "of." It sounded vaguely aristocratic. Dale was nonetheless a reminder that even otherwise perfect Mormon families can be visited with affliction. He was born with a harelip, an abrupt slice in his face that slurred his speech and pulled his mouth toward his nose. At lunch Dale blew milk out of one of his nostrils, a trick he loved to perform.

Harelip or not, Dale was Mormon and comforted by the knowledge that all gentiles were doomed.

I didn't believe in heaven or hell, and had even rejected Santa Claus. Once when I misbehaved just before Christmas my mother threatened that Santa would leave a lump of coal in my stocking, a strange warning, since we had no fireplace and never hung stockings. "There's no such thing as Santa," I said. "I saw Daddy hide the presents in the truck." My mother looked as if she might laugh, but frowned harder and warned me not to tell other children—it would ruin their Christmas. This puzzled me. It seemed wonderful enough that my poor parents would go to the trouble of buying me presents. Why concoct this story about some jolly stranger, for whom it was no sacrifice, dropping gifts on us from out of the sky? But I kept my disbeliefs to myself. Of course Santa was an imaginary creature, and I saw no difference between this old man living at the North Pole and flying around the world giving out presents, and old man God somewhere up in the clouds in heaven letting some in and keeping some out.

At school every morning our teachers read a few verses from the Bible, fantastic stories of floods and whale bellies and prodigal sons and coats of many colors. While my classmates apparently took these as true, Jonah and Joseph were no more real to me than Dick and Jane and their monosyllabic life with Puff and Spot and Mother and Father. I decided believing in God and all those Bible stories somehow just happened when you grew up. That was the real miracle.

None of this stopped me from faking Mormonism. I went to Thursday afternoon "primary" classes and even suffered through Sunday services in Letha, a nearby village with just one paved street, a post office/general store, and the big brick church. Primary was deceptively undemanding religious training. Girls were grouped into classes called "Bluebirds" and "Robins" and "Sunbeams" and told pleasant stories about the Mormon pioneers.

Boys went to another part of the building to prepare for the priesthood. We sang "My Body is a Temple," a vow not to defile ourselves with caffeine and alcohol, and then the boys would come back and we'd all go outside together. The best part of primary was walking to the Letha Store for candy or ice cream. I rose shamelessly through the Sunbeam and Robin ranks, but balked at being baptized. I sensed somehow that this was going too far. My primary teachers, gentle Mormon mothers, just smiled when I said I wasn't ready to join yet. They knew the time was coming when the church would demand some real allegiance.

Mormon Sunday worship was an ordeal, but nothing like the hushed formality of the Presbyterians. Mormon services were noisy and chaotic, with so many crying babies and squirming children crowded into the pews I could barely hear the bishop. Hymnbooks were dropped and retrieved. Pages rustled as we turned to a song. There were whispers and giggles and even an occasional spitball flying through the air. The grownups seemed not to notice. Every once in a while somebody got up to give his testimony about the blessings of the church. I could never quite figure out the order of things, but I knew it was almost over when they brought out the sacrament—platters filled with little silver glasses of grape juice and cubes of white bread. The Mormons let me take this even though I wasn't baptized, another way to bring me closer to conversion. But their sacred ritual was for me an act of private defiance. Big portraits of Jesus and Joseph Smith hung in the front of the chapel, symbols of their equal importance to the Mormons. These men were equally meaningless to me. I gulped my grape juice and glared back at their bland smiling faces, daring them to make me believe.

I pretended religion for the predictable reasons: status and love. There were only two other girls in my grade at school, Janet Morris and LaDonna Fielding. Of course they were both Mormon. The unwritten but unbreakable rule was that you had to have a best friend, and your best friend had to be in your grade. Mormon girls were best friends only with other Mormon girls. Any child could do that math. If I didn't become a Mormon, I could never have an acceptable best friend. I would be like poor Sherry Chapman, who fell in a campfire when she was a baby and had a claw-like deformed hand that nobody would touch: an outcast.

I had a crush on Mark Hansen, a tall, dark-haired boy who looked vaguely like Frankie Avalon. Mark was Mormon, naturally; he was Dale's cousin. Since he went to another country school several miles away, the only place I could see him was at primary. If I didn't become a Mormon, I couldn't have a boyfriend.

Sometimes after primary Mark would walk with me to the Letha Store for a fudgesicle. We rarely spoke, but almost touched hands, barely noticing his little brothers trailing behind, shouting insults and throwing gravel at our backs. We would sit on the wooden steps of the store, savoring our fudgesicles in dreamy silence. This was my secret reward for suffering through boring primary lessons, for pretending to pray to Heavenly Father with my arms folded and head bowed, for chirping out silly children's hymns with the rest of the Robins and Bluebirds.

As a potential convert, a prize yet to be won, I could choose between Janet and LaDonna for my best friend. I tried LaDonna first. A pious little Mormon girl with dark curly hair, she was the oldest of the stairstep Fielding siblings, whose slightly exotic names began either with "L" or "R": LaDonna, Renae, LaMar, Lynnette, Royal, and Rance. All good Mormons had at least six children; Dale told me it was the minimum number to get their parents into heaven. LaDonna's father was a stern patriarch who eyed me skeptically, as if he saw through my ruse. Her mother was soft spoken and patient, the president of Relief Society and a model Mormon woman. She was years younger than my mother but white-haired already, a baby perched on one hip and another tugging on her skirt. One bleak weekend at LaDonna's house was all I could stand.

The Fieldings were even poorer than we were, but they tithed their 10 percent and mercilessly observed Fast Sunday, when all good Mormons, even children, couldn't eat anything between Saturday's noon meal and Sunday dinner. I spent the night with LaDonna before Fast Sunday. We all went to bed early, since there was no dinner to eat and the Fieldings didn't have a television. I shared a cot with LaDonna and Renae, lying awake for hours after they fell asleep. They whimpered sometimes, and their empty stomachs growled. On the other side of the wall in their parents' room, the bedsprings creaked sharply for a few minutes, then fell silent. In the morning Mr. Fielding prayed over an empty breakfast table for us to all be good children of Heavenly Father. Then we crowded into the car and drove to church in silence.

Fast Sunday services were even longer and noisier than usual. An old lady fainted and her family carried her out. The sacrament thimbleful of grape juice and morsel of bread only made me want more. Finally we were released and everyone rushed to their cars. Crowded in the back seat between Renae and LaDonna, I could feel our eagerness: soon now, we would eat. I closed my eyes, imagining roast beef and mashed potatoes, chocolate cake for desert. Mormon women were the best cooks. But Mrs. Fielding served us what they normally had for breakfast—runny softboiled eggs and thin oatmeal, made cold with too much milk. Hungry as I was, I couldn't stomach it. At home I only ate scrambled eggs and put butter and brown sugar on my mush. No one noticed that I just pushed my oatmeal around the bowl and stared at my mucousy eggs. The air was filled with the slurping and swallowing of famished children. Suddenly LaDonna jumped up and ran to the bathroom. She slammed the door, but we could all hear her throwing up.

"I have to go now," I said. Mr. Fielding smiled, happy to dismiss me. I ran all the way back home through the fields, ignoring the piercing pain in my side. The Fieldings were a visceral symbol of what it meant to be a good Mormon. I would have to be best friends with Janet.

Janet's father was a Jack Mormon, an LDS backslider who drank and smoked and swore and never went to church. Janet's big brothers Ross and Danny had dropped out of high school and were Jacks too. Jack Mormons were openly scornful of church teachings, something a gentile would never dare, but still they were accepted by church members in a way the most pious gentile could never be. We all knew it was just a matter of time before a Jack Mormon returned to the fold. Janet's father said goddamn and hell right in front of us and grinned defiantly when he lit up a cigarette or opened a bottle of beer from the refrigerator. Ross and Danny smoked and drank beer too and would probably end up in reform school. They wore their hair in greasy ducktails and mostly worked on their cars, brilliant chrome-covered Chevrolets incongruous as jewels in their muddy barnyard. They grunted and chuckled mysteriously at supper, poking each other in the ribs and grinning over some private joke.

"Looks like the bloody scours," Danny whispered when I poured catsup and mustard on my hamburger.

I stared at the mixture and for the first time saw its resemblance to the terrible diarrhea our calves sometimes got. I would never eat this again.

"Jesus Christ!" Janet's father erupted. "Get the hell away from the table!" Danny and Ross smirked at each other, but pushed their chairs back and sauntered outside to smoke cigarettes. We could hear them through the kitchen window, howling with laughter. Janet's mother just shook her head, embarrassed for everybody. Janet was her only hope for a good Mormon in the family. She would have preferred a staunch LDS girl like LaDonna

Fielding for Janet's best friend, but bringing a gentile like me to the church might make up for all the backsliders in the family. So it was Janet and I who walked smugly arm-in-arm around the school building at recess, leaving LaDonna alone to play with her little sister. She was humiliated, of course, but she knew that good things come to those who wait.

The Daddy Dinner was the social event of the year for the fifth grade primary girls. At the end of the summer we would graduate to "Mutual," the next stage of our indoctrination. The Mutual Improvement Association, held on Wednesday nights, was an opportunity for Mormon teenagers to pair up. There were religion classes for an hour or so, followed by the real motivation for Mutual attendance—a sock-hop dance in the church gymnasium. Other religions viewed the sexual awakening of boys and girls as an unpleasant process, something to be delayed as long as possible, but the Mormons seemed to encourage early romance. We were taught to dance in primary, not the least of the reasons I kept going. The thrill of touching Mark's hand during a Virginia Reel was enough to last me all week. Now Mutual promised even more physical contact.

Janet said the Daddy Dinner would get us ready for real dates. Even her father was going. We were taking our daddies to dinner in the church gym, where we would sit at long tables with real cloth napkins and candles and flowers and eat a meal in courses, prepared for us in the big kitchen. No mothers were allowed, except for a few to bring out the food and do the dishes afterwards.

Until the Daddy Dinner I had been able to keep my parents out of my dishonest association with the Mormons. Going to primary once a week, or to church every so often with Janet and her mother, did not really affect my family. I sometimes wondered why my parents let me risk conversion. My mother never objected, and my father seemed not to notice. Maybe he accepted this as my way to fit into the dominant hostile culture, his immigrant experience revisited. Maybe my mother thought the Presbyterian baptism was as good a vaccination as I could get. Maybe she knew I was bluffing.

Until the Daddy Dinner I was a passive recipient of the religion, only a potential Mormon, a gentile girl being carefully cultivated for church membership. Unbaptized though I was, the Daddy Dinner made me into a missionary, actively recruiting my father to the faith. I forced him that night into a roomful of Mormon men who had rudely ignored him, who smugly looked down on him, who even cheated him in the world outside their church. Mormon farmers had nothing to do with gentile farmers who refused to convert. They did not wave to my father when their pickup trucks passed on the county road. They did not speak to him in narrow aisles of the Letha Store, pointedly saving their smiles and hearty handshakes for the elders in the church. The Mormons ran the only cannery in the county, and we all knew that LDS farmers got a better price for their corn than the gentiles. My father had learned to accept these indignities, and now I was making him sit down with these men, pray with them, and eat their food.

None of this was clear to me then. I only knew how nervous he was, dressed in his only suit, the dark blue one he was married in and the one he wore to funerals, its thin, cheap fabric stretched across his broad shoulders, the sleeves stopping far short of his wrists, his huge farmer hands spreading out from exposed white cuffs. His thick fingers fumbled with the Mormon church silver set so carefully on the bleached white tablecloth before us. I only knew how my face burned when he started to eat before the blessing, then noisily clanked the silver fork down on his plate and folded his big arms in front of his chest the way the rest of us did while LaDonna's daddy asked Heavenly Father to bless this food to our bodies. I only saw how his hand gripped the fork like a shovel, scooping the food into his mouth, how he gulped down his red Mormon punch. How he could only grin anxiously and nod when one of the Mormon men offered to make coolly polite conversation with him, *are you planting sugar beets again this year Art?* How he could only say *uh-huh*, and duck his head shyly, a big Finnish boy among the knowing, disdainful Americans. They smiled sympathetically, approvingly, at me. I was embarrassed for my father but at the same time I knew I had done a terrible thing. I had delivered him to the Mormons. He was enduring this humiliation for the simple reason that I had asked him to and he would do anything for me.

After that night I stopped going to primary, right in the middle of my "Articles of Faith" project—a simple sewing handicraft I could never get quite right. We were supposed to memorize Joseph Smith's thirteen articles, printed on a clear plastic page with holes punched through the edges, while we crocheted a frame around the page. LaDonna Fielding had done hers perfectly. *We believe the Bible to be the Word of God as far as it is translated correctly. We also believe the Book of Mormon to be the Word of God.* For weeks I had fumbled with my crochet needle, making ugly, uneven stitches and pulling them out so often my orange yarn got knotted and dirty. The morning after the Daddy Dinner I found the unfinished project in my closet. *We believe in being honest, true, chaste, benevolent, virtuous, and in doing good to all men.* I crumpled the plastic sheet, ripped out the yarn frame, and threw the whole thing under my bed.

After I quit the church, Renae Fielding called me on the phone, on a mission for her older sister. *LaDonna and Janet hate your guts so you just as well not come to school anymore,* she said. There were giggles in the background. I slammed down the receiver and fled to my room, but didn't cry. I knew I deserved it.

That summer, wading in the irrigation ditch behind our house, I sliced my foot open on a piece of broken glass buried in the mud. Blood streamed into the dirty water, left a red trail through the grass where I ran screaming into the house, puddled horribly on the kitchen floor, soaked through the dishtowel my mother wrapped around my foot before she called the Christian Science practitioner. I clutched the bloody towel and wailed. I could barely hear her frightened voice in the other room, repeating something about knowing the truth. And then the terrible throbbing in my foot faded to almost nothing, a distant memory of pain. Suddenly calm, I peeled back the sodden towel: the wound was jagged and deep but the bleeding had stopped. My mother hung up and hurried back to the kitchen. "It's better," I said, holding up my foot for her to see. And then I waited for an explanation.

Seven

1961: HUNTING AND GATHERING

STEALING IRRIGATION WATER was a terrible crime; poaching was a prank. At the ranch, Uncle Oscar told game warden jokes around the kitchen table, his summer-killed doe hanging in a dark corner of the hayloft. Once he almost got caught. *The sonofabitch was standing right there when I came out of the barn.*

"You been butchering something?" the game warden asked, looking at my uncle's bloody hands.

Oscar grinned. "Just making steers out of bull calves, officer."

The game warden stared at the barn for a long time, like he might see something through the wall. He knew these old Finlanders had no respect for seasons. Oscar stood his ground, never taking his eyes off the other man. *Ah, to hell with it,* the game warden said finally, and stomped back to his state truck.

Every September my father and his brothers went elk hunting in the back country and practiced a communal use of tags: everybody brought home an elk whether he shot it or not. These two-week expeditions, the only real vacations my father ever had, took months of planning and always made for a good story afterwards. Once they camped downstream from a dead horse in the creek and didn't discover the bloated carcass until they'd been there a week, using water from the defiled stream. Another year my father shot a rare mountain goat way back in Chamberlain Basin and couldn't resist mounting the horns on our garage. There wasn't even a season on goats. I held my breath every time somebody remarked on the tiny spiked rack: *where'd you get that, Art?* He would smile mischievously, mumbling something about buying it off an old timer in Long Valley. Nobody believed him, but everybody laughed.

Late in the fall he hunted the nearby riverbottom sloughs, thick with cattails and mallards. He didn't stop shooting until the back of his pickup was knee-deep with ducks. I learned to hate the muddy taste of the meat; even ground into a black paste and mixed with mayonnaise it was horrible. Flying livers, my cousin Roger called them. Roger could always make me laugh.

The best tasting wild birds were the Chinese ringneck pheasants that lived right in our fields. Riding my horse on summer mornings, I might scare up a brown-flecked hen and a dozen or more pheasant chicks, erupting in a flurry of wings. Brilliant cocks always rose with an indignant crow, two discordant syllables, the sun glinting off their iridescent feathers. Once a fleeing chick slammed right into the barbed wire fence and fell back to the ground. I found the tiny body in the weeds. Its eyes were shut, but I could see its heart beating under its downy breast feathers, and in its throat, a tiny bloodless hole—the prick of a single barb. I put the chick inside my jacket pocket, imagining an exotic pet, but in a few minutes it regained pheasant consciousness and began to struggle frantically. I gathered him up in my hand. The tiny bird stared back at me, a terrifying giant who could crush him in an instant. I sighed and tossed the chick high into the air. He flew straight away, his miniature wings making a feathery drill in the still morning air. The summer I was eleven a ringneck rooster took up residence in the field outside my bedroom window and cackled like clockwork at dawn. I saw him just once.

Pheasant season lasted just a few weeks in the fall, and for that brief period the farm was an exciting, desirable place. Our relatives would drive from as far away as Portland to be there for opening day. It became a ritual: around 10 o'clock, strange cars began filling up the driveway and there were hearty greetings and steaming coffee and sweet rolls served outside on the pickup tailgates. My father and uncles and boy cousins would kill time cleaning their shotguns and checking their watches, grinning at each other. Their bird dogs whined and trembled, smelling gun oil and the gun powder inside red and green shell casings and dried blood on hunting vests from years past.

The season began exactly at noon and for the first few hours it sounded like a guerilla war. On farms all over the valley unsuspecting pheasants flew up and into the sights of shotguns. Boom! Those beautiful birds, fat from eating our wheat and corn all summer, suddenly found the sky filled with buckshot. The dogs were delighted—my father's ruthless English pointer Butch, who killed field mice and cats in the off-season; Uncle Raymond's black lab Mac, so friendly he always seemed to be smiling; my cousin Roger's Brittany Spaniel, Lady, who had the keenest nose of the three but shivered all the time and cowered if you spoke too loud.

The first birds to die on opening day were reckless young roosters, some not even fully colored, cut down in pheasant adolescence. Shooting hens was illegal except on the last Sunday of the season, but sometimes it was hard to tell and sometimes it was just too tempting. They taste just the same, the hunter would grin, stuffing a hen into the back of his vest. When we got back to the truck the bird was shoved way underneath the seat, just in case we ran into a Fish and Game roadblock while on the way to hunt on another farm.

Because I was a girl, I did not hunt. But I could walk behind the hunters, carry their dead roosters, and watch the dogs work. By late afternoon on opening day the surviving pheasants were harder to find, hunkered down in weedy ditches or hiding in the uncut cornfields. Sweet corn had been harvested long before hunting season, but field corn, winter feed for cattle, wasn't chopped into silage until late fall. The drying stalks still stood in towering rows, a perfect pheasant refuge in a deadly flat landscape. This was where girls came in handy. The hunters would wait at one end of a field while my girl cousins and I walked toward them through the rows of corn, pushing pheasants in their direction. We knew we'd done well when a bird flew up somewhere in front of us, and seconds later, gunshots. Sometimes we would get peppered with stray buckshot and scream dramatically, but it was all part of the hunt. A stinging bb just made the job more exciting.

The withered cornstalks were way over our heads. Walking down a row, I couldn't see anything but drooping yellow leaves and papery cornhusks and dried cornsilk hanging down like limp hair. Fall sunlight dappled the ground, and it was so quiet sometimes I imagined this was a magical forest, like in a fairy tale. Deep in my reverie, I once almost stepped on a pheasant, but he refused to fly. It was a big ringneck rooster with bronzy blue and green breastfeathers and a magnificent long tail. He looked right at me as if to say, *you will have to kill me here.* I could hear one of my girl cousins a few rows away, humming to herself and casually breaking down the brittle stalks in her path. We were getting close to the end of the field—the hunter's genial voices floated above us in the still air. I smiled and backed away from the defiant bird. Nobody needed to know.

My cousin Roger was a crack shot even though he was only two years older than me. His family lived in Horseshoe Bend and used to drive down to the farm every month or so. His dad, my mother's brother Charles, owned a ranch in the foothills where the Payette River made a U-shaped turn that gave the town its name. In summer they ran cattle in the timber above the ranch. From the time he was five years old, Roger got to go with his father and their hired cowhands to move the herd up to the high country. Now he could rope a calf and brand and dehorn just like a man. He bragged that he was shaving already. Roger had a powerful quarter horse named Buster that I was afraid to ride.

My brother and I loved for Roger to visit. He had a silly side he only showed to us. Roger could entertain us just by riding my

The author with Silver and her brother on his rocking horse, 1959

old rocking horse and pretending it was running away with him. "Whoa, Silver! Whoa!" he'd scream, and he looked so ridiculous, straddling that wooden toy, his knees dragging the ground, his eyes wide in mock fear. The foolish-looking rocking horse, with its painted blue eyes and scalloped wooden mane, was a perfect prop. Roger had worked up a whole routine. He would pretend to sneak up on the wooden horse, leap on its back, and rock furiously, arms and legs flailing the air. Soon Steve and I were breathless from laughing and begging him to stop. Whenever Uncle Charles drove in we'd run to the car and plead with Roger to ride the rocking horse for us.

One Sunday afternoon in July, Uncle Charles and Roger came to get a gunny sack of sweet corn before the cannery picker came. There is nothing better than buttered new corn, picked when it's just turning yellow, the kernels still small and tender. While my father and Charles went to the cornfield we stayed in the yard so Roger could put on his rocking horse show for us. It was even more hilarious than usual, and my sides were aching from laughing when my mother called out the kitchen window that it was time to milk the Jersey.

This was one of my chores since my father sold his dairy herd. The Jersey was our only milk cow and we didn't need a machine for just her. She was small, and so gentle I could milk her right in the corral if I wanted. She never kicked. I liked the rhythmic splash in the shiny stainless steel bucket, the foam rising up almost hot and smelling sweet. I would lean my head against the Jersey's soft brown flank and gently grasp her rubbery teats, feeling the milk work its way out. The barn cats came around then, mewing and twitching their tails, rubbing their skinny bodies against my legs.

Roger said he'd go with me. Our shadows stretched out long behind us in the late afternoon slant of the sun. I dug my toes into the soft warm dust. Roger's pointy cowboy boots made deep triangles and square heel marks in the dust next to my barefoot prints. Clouds were plumping up like feathery pillows on the horizon, getting ready to make a glorious sunset. I carried the milk bucket, feeling the cool metal brush against my bare leg as I walked.

Roger got ahead of me and disappeared inside the barn. I was in no particular hurry; I knew the Jersey would be waiting for me in the pasture.

I stepped into the barn darkness, breathing in the pungent smells of old wood and dried cow manure and hay, all mixed into something almost pleasant. It took a moment for my eyes to adjust and see that Roger was a few steps ahead when his cupped hand swung back and caught me firmly between my legs. He held on for a moment, then let go. Roger turned his head and looked right at me, smiling strangely. Then he sauntered outside. I couldn't move, trying to understand what just happened, if something had happened. Dust motes floated in the sunlight pouring through the cracks in the old barn walls. The little brown bottles of my father's calf medicines were lined up on a high shelf, just like always. The Jersey's wooden milking stall was open, ready for our peaceful routine. Everything must be all right.

But when Roger opened the gate to the pasture the Jersey backed away. Her nostrils flared and her eyes widened. "Come on, you stupid cow!" Roger shouted. Instead she turned and lumbered off, her full bag bouncing between her back legs.

She's never done this before I said, hurrying past Roger to head her off. I got in front of the loping cow, and was just turning her back when she stopped at a weak place in the fence. The Jersey looked at me for a moment, then pushed through the sagging wire and disappeared into the sweet corn. I was in trouble now.

Without thinking I scrambled through the fence and pushed into the towering cornstalks. It was stifling inside, a sweaty combination of trapped summer heat and the field's own green moisture. I tried to run down a corrugate, but the corn's blade-like leaves overlapped and sliced at my bare legs. Spiky tassels at the tops of the stalks swayed in my wake and rained down sticky grains.

The Jersey was somewhere in front of me, knocking down the corn in horrible loud crashes. I stopped for a minute to figure out which way she was going. It was not hard to tell; the cow sounded like a whole herd. I headed desperately in her direction, sharp green blades cutting my arms and face, tassel dust prickling my skin. Finally I saw the Jersey's tawny form just ahead. She had stopped, head down and panting, exhausted from her escape. If I could just grab hold of her halter....

I heard another crashing come nearer—Roger. Good, I thought, forgetting everything but catching the Jersey. The two of us could bring her back for sure. "Over here! I called, and heard him pushing through the corn to us. Then I could see him, his face, that strange smile, coming right for me, and when the Jersey suddenly bolted and ran away, so did I.

Now there were three of us crashing through the field, the Jersey somewhere ahead, me, and Roger close behind. I veered off just to be sure, and he followed. I could hear him breathing, hear his boots hit the soft dirt, feel his hand on my shoulder, pulling me back. My head was on the ground, looking up at the brilliant blue sky far above. Roger was bending over me, grinning, panting. His hands were holding my shoulders down. I felt disconnected; my head was here, my shoulders there, my legs and feet somewhere else, and Roger's smiling face loomed over me like the moon.

Somehow I wrenched backward under his grasp, pulled my right leg up and slammed at him hard with my bare foot. Roger cried out in surprise and seemed to leap backwards. Then he lay curled up like a baby, holding his knees to his chest, eyes squeezed shut. For a second I could only stare at this strange, clenched form. Then I jumped to my feet, jolted by rage. I wasn't afraid now, not at all. I wanted to say something that would hurt him so much more and for so much longer than a kick in the groin. He opened his eyes and looked at me, still grimacing in pain. I took a ragged breath.

"Why don't you grow up?" was the worst I could hiss at him. My voice sounded high and thin; the words were so silly and unworthy of what I felt.

Even crumpled on the ground, he managed a scornful smile.

"Why don't you?" he said, ugly and hoarse.

I turned and ran through the corn, heedless now of the slicing leaves. Finally I reached the edge of the field, not far from where we all had gone in. Through the gathering dusk I could see the Jersey back in the pasture, grazing peacefully. She raised her

head and looked at me, then turned and walked calmly toward the barn.

I didn't know what else to do but the milking. It was dark when I turned the cow back out into the pasture and lugged the sloshing bucket back to the house. Uncle Charles's car was gone. My mother and father were sitting at the kitchen table drinking coffee. Nobody spoke. I sat the milk bucket on the counter. "I need to take a bath," I said, afraid to look at them.

I filled the tub with water as hot as I could stand and slowly lowered myself in. I looked at my body as if it belonged to someone else.

It was thin and hard, a flat child's chest, skinny arms and legs, knobby knees. Dried blood hatchmarked the arms. Dirt clumped under the fingernails, between the toes. I sank as low as I could, until my hair floated around my face like weeds, my nose and mouth just above the grimy water.

The bathroom door opened and my mother came in. She dropped the lid on the toilet and sat down.

"What happened?" she said. "Your face is all scratched."

"The Jersey ran into the cornfield. Had to go get her." I stared at the ceiling, refusing to meet her gaze.

"You and Roger?"

I nodded.

"And he almost caught her when she kicked him?"

So that's what he told them.

"Is that what happened?"

I nodded again, slowly. But I felt hot tears sliding down my face.

My mother shook her head. She bent toward me, her eyes hard and disbelieving, hands clenched on her lap.

"The truth," she said. "Tell me."

"He—he tried," I whispered. "But nothing happened. Honest. I got away."

She closed her eyes and sighed. Pure relief.

"Okay," she said. "We can't tell your father. He'd kill him. But you're all right now. Nobody else needs to know."

She pulled a clean bath towel from the shelf and dropped it next to the tub.

"You'd better get out soon," she called cheerfully, loud enough so my father could hear. "It's getting late."

She started to leave, but stopped at the door, her hand gripping the white porcelain knob.

"In a little while you will forget all about this," she said, so softly I could barely hear. "You won't think about it at all."

Then she was gone.

I lay motionless in the water until it started to feel cold. Then I pulled the bathtub plug up with my toes and waited until all the dirty water had gurgled noisily down the drain pipe. I was suddenly so tired.

The pheasant cackled loudly at dawn, but this time I was ready. I jumped out of bed and opened my window even before the sound had faded. There he was, much closer than I'd imagined, a splash of bronze in the dewy green hayfield. He looked right at me, cocked his head, and broke the still morning with another jagged, jubilant crow. I laughed. The ringneck noisily ruffled his feathers, then turned and strutted away, his long tail feathers trailing the ground. I watched until he disappeared in the dense cover.

Eight

1962: LABOR LAWS

OUR CROPS WERE FAT from fertilizer and constant care, from pesticide sprays and relentless watering and, for the sugar beets, hoeing weeds twice each summer. Sugar beets might grow to the size of small boulders by October's harvest, but the young plants were almost precious, requiring the attention of a gardener, to be hoed by hand.

This job was so terrible only Mexicans would do it. They came to the farm early in the morning, standing in the backs of big open trucks, and descended on our fields like guerilla forces armed with hoes. They wore sweaty straw hats, round-toed work boots, and tattered, filthy clothes that seemed either too big or too small. For a time I imagined that they were exotic and even dangerous, laughing and jostling each other and talking fast in an incomprehensible language, paying no attention to me standing in the yard, staring shamelessly.

I was almost a teenager and had seen only one Mexican up close in my life, a girl named Juanita who sat across from me for a few weeks in the fourth grade. Our valley was ringed with big orchards—apples, cherries, plums, and pears—all the jump-rope rhyme fruits, harvested by Mexicans and itinerant whites and local kids needing summer jobs. We even had a Cherry Festival with a queen and a parade and a carnival. Juanita's family was picking apples, the last crop to come in, and for some reason they sent her to school. Most Mexicans kept their kids working right alongside them, but on the first day of school Juanita was standing on the edge of the highway in front of the labor camp, looking like she was waiting for something in her puff-sleeved pink dress and white patent leather shoes, gripping a lunch sack in front of her. The driver wasn't used to stopping there so he drove right past, then slammed on the breaks, throwing us forward in our seats. We shouted our collective disapproval while he ground the gears into reverse and backed up for Juanita. When he swung the door open in her face she just stood there, biting on her lip. Everybody got quiet, watching. Finally she climbed in and sat in the empty seat right behind the driver, always the last place to be taken. At school Juanita gave the principal a folded piece of paper that said what her name was and that she was in the fourth grade.

She was the biggest girl in our class. The elasticized puffy sleeves of her dress cut into her muscular upper arms, leaving red lines in her brown skin. The bodice was tight around her thick chest. She was even growing breasts. Obviously Juanita's mother did not know that puff-sleeves and patent leather were not what girls wore in the fourth grade. My favorite outfit was a boat-necked blue sweater, pedal pushers, and slip-on Keds canvas shoes. The principal brought Juanita into our room. He talked quietly to our teacher, Mrs. Smalley, who pursed her thin lips and scowled. She told Juanita to sit across from me, in what would have been Francine Rainey's desk except her family had moved to Arizona over the summer.

It was the one I wanted. Our old oak desks were really two separate pieces: armless chairs and broad sloping desktops, each set on scrolly iron legs. The hinged desktops opened up so you could put your books inside, and the hinged seats closed up so somebody could raise yours while you went to the pencil sharpener or the bathroom. When you came back if you weren't watching you'd sit down and fall on the floor. All the metal legs were bolted to a pair of long board runners so that entire rows of desks could only be moved all at once. The best desks were like Juanita's—with the desk part at the end of one set of runners and the chair at the beginning of another set. In this junction, if you pushed your feet really hard against the desktop legs, the whole row would slide forward on its runners, and you could slump way down in the seat so the teacher couldn't see you, stretching out your legs in the newly opened space. Or you could hook your feet inside the metal scrolls and pull the row closer, pull the desktop in so tight to your body you couldn't move. With a desk like that, there was always something to do. I was going to ask Mrs. Smalley if I could move to Francine's old place when she told Juanita to sit there. After that, nobody wanted it.

Juanita was never called on and she never raised her hand. I realized later I had never heard her speak. She seemed to read to herself; I would glance over sometimes and catch her mouthing words in a book. She concentrated so hard on writing that she broke her pencil points, a snap! in the enforced silence of our afternoon penmanship. Mrs. Smalley scolded Juanita for using the pencil sharpener too much.

At lunchtime we'd gather in groups on the cement slab in front of the school. Juanita sat back by herself on the steps, munching mournfully on something that looked like beans rolled up in a pancake. We ate bologna and mayonnaise sandwiches and potato chips wrapped in wax paper, drank tepid milk or Kool-Aid from our Roy Rogers and Davey Crockett thermos bottles, and negotiated careful trades: oranges for apples, oatmeal cookies for creme-filled Oreos or spicy gingersnaps. We would barter everything but candy bars or pomegranates. Candy was too expensive and pomegranates were too rare, never traded, grudgingly shared with only your best friend. Pomegranates required more work than other fruit. You had to tear back the reddish mottled rind and carefully mine the honeycomb pulp for bits of ruby fruit. Pomegranates were wasteful—even inside the translucent morsels there were seeds to spit out. But they were strangely delicious, tart and spicy at the same time. A pomegranate was nothing like the fleshy bland peaches or the fat sweet cherries our orchards were famous for. A pomegranate grew somewhere far away, in California or maybe even some other country, where pleasure was not measured by volume, but intensity.

Every day after finishing her bean-filled pancake, Juanita would miraculously produce a pomegranate from the wrinkled lunch sack. Her brown fingers dug into the pulp and crammed the fruit into her mouth. She apparently swallowed the seeds. We all watched her, the red pomegranate juice on her hands and at the corners of her mouth, but nobody ever thought to ask her to share.

One stifling afternoon we were working on penmanship, my worst subject, doing the hard letters—q and z. The room was so quiet I could hear the flies buzzing against the windows, the scratch of my pencil lead against the paper. Then, something else: a dripping sound. I turned my head to locate the noise when the drip turned to a trickle, running off the seat of Juanita's chair and splashing on the varnished hardwood floor below. The other kids heard it too. Realization widened their eyes, and they stared, aghast, at Mrs. Smalley. Our teacher sat red faced and furious behind her desk, but not looking at Juanita, not looking at any of us. She fixed her gaze on the ceiling. Was she praying? Her hands gripped the edge of her big oak desk as if it might rise into the air. I was holding my breath, waiting for the terrible splashing to stop. Finally the trickle slowed to a few drops, and then silence. Mrs. Smalley turned her head to see the clock; we all looked too. It was 1:30—an hour until recess.

Go outside until I call you back in, Mrs. Smalley said. At first nobody moved. Did she say we could leave? Mrs. Smalley stood up, her hands still clenching the desk. "Go outside now," she repeated, surveying us all with her hard, mean eyes. *"Now!"* We jumped up and pushed each other to the door, down the hall, into the glaring afternoon. Juanita stayed in her seat. I turned back to look and saw her sitting statue-still, tears squeezing out of her

closed eyes. We heard later that Mrs. Smalley summoned the jani-
tor and took Juanita into the bathroom while he mopped up the
floor and washed off the chair seat. When we came back the
whole room smelled of ammonia, and the clean floor glistened
under Juanita's desk.

After that she was gone. Her chair remained empty the
whole rest of the year, until it was shuffled into a new arrangement and nobody could tell which one it was.

I thought about Juanita whenever the Mexicans came to hoe
beets—was one of them her father, her brother? I knew they all
lived in labor camps, bleak cinder block buildings with no running water or inside toilets, and they were trucked to our farms
like cattle. I had seen a TV show about migrant workers and how
terrible their lives were, but still I was more intrigued than sym-
pathetic. These were not the sunburned farmboy haying crews
who lived down the road and ate dinner in the house and teased
me good-naturedly when I poured their iced tea. These dark
skinned men came from unimaginably far away and couldn't
even speak English and would never step inside our door. They
made our farm feel like a foreign country.

When the Mexicans were safely out in the beet field I would
move close enough to eavesdrop on my father and the crew boss
while they leaned up against his truck and smoked cigarettes.
Their cigarette smoke and the unwashed scent of the Mexicans
hung in the warm morning air. I listened to them talk and
watched the Mexicans moving up and down the rows, heads bent,
chopping at the ground.

"They have one speed: slow," my father joked to the crew
boss.

The crew boss was not a Mexican, but he drove the truck and
negotiated the price of weeding; my father paid him and he paid
them.

"Yeah," he replied, "but they can keep it up all day."

After a while I might go in and watch television or read but sooner or later I was back outside, standing on the top rail of the corral and shading my eyes to see them better. By noon the relentless summer sun made everything so bright it hurt just to keep looking. They didn't seem to take time off for lunch. The air grew heavy and still and nothing moved in the glaring heat but the Mexicans going slowly, methodically down one row and up another, upending bushy pigweeds, hacking at the tough ropey roots of wild geraniums, slicing through Canadian thistles thicker than my arm. The afternoon air shimmered between us.

Finally I would retreat to my parents' bedroom. My father had stuck a swamp cooler in the window and hooked up a hose to the back. I loved lying in the darkened room right next to the cooler, its motor roaring, well water from the hose running down the back of the cooler and pooling in the bottom. The air rushed out so cool and moist. I would put my face right next to the fan, separated from the spinning blades by just a screen mesh, and let the wet wind lap against my cheeks and blow my hair straight back. I could hear the water dripping down inside the cooler, and if I closed my eyes and ignored the droning motor I could imagine a cool cave, an underground waterfall, stalactites and stalagmites piercing the shadows like ancient swords. Just a few feet from the fan the air grew warm and sweaty, and outside the bedroom the cooler had no effect at all. But I could lie on the edge of the bed and be in the path of a narrow band of caressing air. It rippled over my skin, thick with water, taking me far away from the baking heat outside.

The summer I was twelve, just out of the seventh grade, I convinced my father to let me hoe one narrow little beet field for money. Other kids I knew got to pick cherries or plums or thin apples, making enough to buy their school clothes in Boise. But my mother went to summer school to keep up her teaching certificate and my father was busy all day irrigating or working on machinery or doctoring cattle; he had no time to drive me to the work in the orchards. So I begged him to let me hoe that one little beet field, only fourteen acres and most of that in the length, and he said yes. I just had to finish before the Mexicans came to do the other fields.

I had figured out how much I would make, more than $50, and I wouldn't have to leave home and pick cherries at four cents a pound to do it. It was enough to buy a Bobbi Brooks coulotte outfit, a ribbed poor boy sweater, and matching kneesocks—wonderful clothes I saw in *Seventeen*, on smiling blond models whose lives were so much better than mine. Without the money I would have to wear what my mother could afford in the cut-rate department store in town, clothes that tried to look like the good ones but weren't, the style not quite right or the material too thin and wrinkly, with seams that split in the first washing, buttons that fell off in your hand. I wanted something better.

I started hoeing the beet field at dawn, wearing one of my father's straw hats and a pair of his gloves, my blue jean cut-offs, and a sleeveless shirt. I was already tanned from swimming in the canal, and didn't have to worry about the sun. I put my lunch and a thermos jug of water at the far end of the field, an incentive to keep me going. At first I worked fast to take advantage of the coolest part of the day. The weeds were gigantic, fertilized indiscriminately along with the sugar beets. I chopped at Canadian thistles as big as trees, wild geraniums running indefinitely along the ground, pigweeds taller than I was. Furiously I hacked away at their roots, clouds of dust rising from my hoe. The weeds became my enemies. It wasn't long before I felt my arms and back beginning to hurt. Sweat mixed with dust and ran down my face in muddy streams. My exposed skin itched from the pigweed pollen, was scratched by prickly thistles. My legs felt weak. I tried to keep myself from looking for the end of the row, so impossibly distant. Still I kept working, forcing myself to think of all the clothes I could buy with the money I was making. Poor boy sweaters, pleated skirts, Madras plaid blouses. Hip-hugger pants with wide belts. I kept going, up one row, then down the other, just as I had seen the Mexicans do. Finally it was noon. I dragged myself to the corner of the field where my lunch waited and sat on the ditch-bank, eating without pleasure or satisfaction. I had worked more than six hours, and had finished only four rows. There were at least forty in the field, narrow as it was. If I did four more today, and eight a day after that, it would take me five days in all. I thought about the *Seventeen* models in their perfect clothes, their perfect lives. Five days was not so long. I could do it.

By early afternoon I had a headache from the glaring sun and broiling heat. The weeds loomed taller and thicker; some-times when I swung the hoe it bounced back, mocking me. I was startled to see that my arms were bright red. Pain spread up my back and into my shoulders. My feet throbbed. I could hear noth-ing but buzzing insects and my own dry-mouthed breathing, and longed to just lie down in the grass at the end of the row. Finally I looked at my watch. Two-thirty. I had finished one row and was halfway down the next, but could no longer lift the hoe. In the middle of the afternoon, in the middle of the fifth of forty rows, I sank to the ground, exhausted. I rested my forehead on my knees, feeling sweat trickle down my back. My arms and face burned; my legs quivered. The little beet field had won.

I dragged myself to the house. My father was in the kitchen getting a glass of water. He looked at me and grinned, a mixture of sympathy and I told you so in his expression.

Hot out there, he said. I could only nod my head.

He took a long drink and set his glass down on the counter.

"It's hard work, sissie," he said, the nickname he used when I needed comforting. "I would have been surprised if you did it." He tried patting me gently on the shoulder but I winced. "You got a bad sunburn," he said, eyeing my bright red arms. "Why don't you get cleaned up and lay down? Mom'll be home from school soon and start supper."

In the bathroom I slowly pulled off my dirty clothes and examined the damage. My shoulders and arms felt like they were on fire and my palms were rubbed raw from the hoe handle. There were big blisters on my feet. The bathwater stung like alcohol and I couldn't bear soap or even a washcloth. When I got out of the tub I slathered Noxema on my arms and face, put on a thin nightgown, and limped into my parents' bedroom, where the swamp cooler droned. I lay down on the bed, closed my eyes, and let the cool air wash over me. I was a princess kept in a cave, waiting to be rescued. I was a cheerleader. I was popular. I was rich.

After a couple of weeks I could peel off patches of sunburned skin without flinching, and the blisters on my hands and feet shrank away. Then my back didn't hurt any more. When the Mexicans came back and hoed my field in half a day, I stayed inside the house until they were gone. They no longer interested me.

First grade

Fifth grade

Ninth grade

Nine

1963: BEAUTY AND TRUTH

J ANET GREW BREASTS IN THE SIXTH GRADE. LaDonna got them in seventh. But I was thirteen and still flat as a board, *just like an ironing board with two peas on it*, I heard Mickey Garner whisper when I walked by. "Stick shape!" Dale Hansen called to me on the playground. I felt like puking. They knew.

Every morning I examined my chest, searching for some sign of change. Every morning it was as hard and fleshless as before, with barely a dimple between my nipples. And then I would put on my Maidenform circle stitch bra, size 28AA, and stuff a nylon stocking into each empty cup. Nylons were much better than Kleenex, which made a humiliating crunch, a sound like walking in snow, if someone bumped up against you. Nylons felt softer and less lumpy. I plumped my bra cups like pillows and got dressed, pleading with the deity to at least let me develop before ninth grade. Ninth grade meant riding the bus to town and junior high. It meant changing classes, eating lunch downtown at Sander's Fountain, sock hops in the gym on Fridays. But most of all it meant going to PE, a required class. And in PE you had to take showers.

I had heard all about this from Linda Thompson and Connie Wallace, girls a year older than me. In PE you had to wear a white blouse and shorts and you had to take off all your clothes, every day, and get in a big shower room with a bunch of other naked girls. You could only be excused when you had your period. Mrs. Gussey was very strict. Linda and Connie watched my face closely for a reaction. They knew.

For more than a year I anticipated ninth grade with growing, gut-twisting dread. So far I had been able to keep up the pretense.

I stopped swimming in public after my mom took us to the pool at Roystone Hot Springs and a nylon floated out of my suitfront. I didn't stay all night with anybody or have anybody spend the night with me. I had come to regard my flat chestedness as an irrevocable deformity, like Dale Hansen's harelip or Sherry Chapman's burned up hand. I tried everything to make my breasts grow: sleeping on my back, not wearing tight clothes, even special exercises. I prayed, begged, pleaded with God to give me even little ones, something! But my body remained stubbornly a child's, and the months until junior high melted away.

When I was eleven I read in a movie magazine about the actor Robert Mitchum causing a big scandal when he kissed some carhop's breast through her tight sweater. That was the beginning of my despair. The story was in an old *Photoplay* that Phyllis, our live-in Christian Science "housekeeper," threw away. I never learned where Phyllis came from or why my mother brought her home. Nobody I knew had a housekeeper, and Phyllis did not do any work that I could see. She mostly stayed in the spare bedroom, reading or playing with her baby. Phyllis apparently had no husband. She nursed the baby right in front of us, amazing me and embarrassing my father. I had never before seen a woman's bare breast in real life.

There were pictures of naked Negro women in the *National Geographic*s at my piano teacher's house, but they didn't count. Even Daisy Mae in the Sunday comics, her curvy bosom outlined beneath her low-cut, polka-dotted blouse, was more exciting. It was the Robert Mitchum story, with its blurry photograph of some man's head bent over some girl's bosom, that for some reason made me breathless. It was dawning on me, the importance of breasts. I watched the Miss America pageant on television, focusing on the contestants' chests: those perfect fleshy cones sticking out in front of them, holding up their strapless gowns and pushing out the fronts of their bathing suits. All my favorite shows became a relentless source of breasts: the girls who danced on *American Bandstand* bounced them under their Peter Pan blouses, Miss Kitty on *Gunsmoke* had them in her fancy saloon gown, even Betty in her shirtwaist dresses on *Father Knows Best* had what was euphemistically called "a good figure" if you looked close enough. Not to mention Sophia Loren, Gina Lollabrigida, Marilyn Monroe, Jane Mansfield—sultry Italians and beaming platinum blondes whose astounding bosoms had made them rich and famous. Their pictures were on the covers of Phyllis's magazines. They were leaning back, laughing, arching their backs, proud and disdainful. I realized that the world was divided into two groups—women who had bosoms and those who didn't. And those who didn't, had nothing.

I clipped a newspaper story about two girls, sixteen and still flat chested, who committed suicide together by jumping off a bridge in Oklahoma. They left a note that said they didn't want to live if they weren't going to develop. This made perfect sense to me. But since I wasn't sixteen yet, I decided to wait. I would try the Mark Eden Bust Developer first.

In the back of all the *Photoplay* magazines was an advertisement for the mysterious Bust Developer. The ad didn't show a picture of the device, just "before" and "after" pictures of women who had used it. Their miraculous new chests would be well worth the $9.95 plus shipping and handling, a huge sum I finally saved from my lunch money and cleaning houses for neighbors. The Bust Developer came with a money-back guarantee. If you weren't satisfied with the results you could return it for a full refund. The advertisement said the Developer would arrive in a plain brown wrapper, so nobody would know. When a little brown package came in the mail, my father examined it curiously. "I don't know what this is," he said, handing it to me. I refused to look at him. I grabbed the box and ran to my room, tearing it open in my closet where nobody could see. Inside was something that looked like a pink plastic clam, its shells about the size of my hands. A heavy spring separated the open clamshells. You were supposed to put it between your palms, arms bent slightly in front of you, and press your hands together to force the clamshell shut. I tried it. The spring made a loud creak. I couldn't see how this would get me a bosom, but the directions said that if I used it regularly for six weeks, I'd have a bust just like the women in the ads—or I could return it for a full refund.

All through eighth grade I frantically exercised, pushing my palms rhythmically against the pink plastic, compressing the spring with a noisy screak that my parents must have heard outside my bedroom door. But nothing happened to my body. I had known all along it was hopeless. Finally I sneaked the thing into my father's machine shop and smashed it to pink shards with his sledge hammer. That was the most satisfaction Mark Eden ever gave me.

I graduated eighth grade valedictorian with straight A's and got to give a speech at the ceremony. None of this mattered. I was flat as ever and spent the summer dreading September.

In junior high you got a different report card for every class. The first ones came in mid-October. Your parents had to sign on the back.

"What's this?" My mother called, her voice angry. "Come here!"

I walked into the room slowly, stone-faced, steeling myself.

She was holding my report cards at arm's length, trying to get me to take them. I stared up at the ceiling instead.

"What is this *D*?" she shrieked, yanking the offending yellow card from the pack and slamming it down on the kitchen table. "You got a *D* in physical education? Is this right?"

I glared back at her but said nothing. She would not understand. Nobody could.

She shuffled through the other cards, reading my grades aloud. "English—A, Algebra—B, Home Ec—A minus; World Geography—B plus." Then back to the bottom of the deck.

"A *D* in PE! Your easiest class!" My mother slammed the cards down hard. "This doesn't make any sense! You're a perfectly normal, healthy girl!"

"I. . . am. . .not!" I screamed, the words coming out separately, an enraged breath for each one. "I am not normal!"

And then I ran to my room and slammed the door, hurling myself facedown on the bed. I did not cry. This pain was beyond tears.

I had faked having a period for as long as I could, claimed to be sick, and simply skipped class, but by October the confrontation finally came between me and Mrs. Gussey, our shapely PE teacher. Everybody said she looked just like Sandra Dee. Mrs. Gussey stood over me in the locker room, her hands on her curvy hips, her pink mouth pursed in a frown.

"Now I want you to get in that shower," she said. "We've had enough of this nonsense. Everybody else showers, and you will too."

I huddled on the wooden bench, my hands over my face. I could hear the other girls giggling. They knew.

"Now," she repeated. "Get undressed."

Let me die, let me die, let me die, I prayed. *If you can't give me breasts, then at least let me be dead.* Mrs. Gussey may have looked like Gidget in her tight white shorts and midi blouse, but she had the personality of a drill sergeant. I expected her to grab me and start pulling off my clothes. I imagined her jerking nylon stockings out of my bra, tossing them on the floor. The other girls would laugh hysterically, chanting the terrible word: *falsies! falsies!*

It was so quiet I could hear the shower dripping, echoing off the concrete walls. I could hear Mrs. Gussey's sharp breathing.

But I didn't move. She understood that she would have to drag me off that bench.

"All right girls," she called. "Get back to your own business!" Amazingly, she stomped away. I heard locker doors open and slam shut; chirpy voices rose. The familiar sounds of girls getting dressed and gossiping swirled around me. Then the bell erupted in a buzzing drill, and the other girls swarmed out of the room, laughing and shouting good-byes to each other. Finally it was quiet. I lifted my head.

Lana Bright, a Horseshoe Bend girl with a bad reputation, was leaning up against the wall, eyeing me. Lana had big breasts and a huge ratted hairstyle made rock-hard with Rayette hairspray. She was going steady with a boy who worked at the mill. Every Monday she came to school with splotchy purple hickeys on her neck, like birthmarks. Lana smoked cigarettes in the park across the street from school and gave teachers the finger when they weren't looking. She was alternately rumored to be pregnant, to have a baby, to be married. She had never spoken to me.

"Not bad," Lana said, arching one black penciled eyebrow and almost smiling at me. "You made that blond bitch back down. Wanna go have a smoke?"

I shook my head miserably. I understood there was a penalty for my defiance. I would never make Honor Society, and I would never have breasts either. It was because I wanted them too much.

Ten

1955-1964: HORSEPOWER

I LIVED IN IDAHO but not the West. This was no silly riddle—
when is a door not a door?—but a mystical truth unrelated to
geography. The question was how to escape. *When it's ajar.*

The West demanded a ranch. My father first bought forty,
then the adjoining forty, and finally eighty more acres, but a cultivated quarter section is still just a farm. Real ranches stretched
for miles untended, with splashing creeks instead of muddy ditches,
natural springs instead of ponds that dried up in winter. Ranch-
ers disdained the monotony of milking cows and instead raised
beef cattle, Black Angus or white-faced Herefords with a hulking
range bull to seed the calf crop. Our placid Holsteins were artifi-
cially inseminated by the "bull man" from the Dairymen's Association. He wore a white coat and looked a little like a doctor.
Farm cows spent their whole lives in filthy corrals and fenced pastures and never knew any better. Ranch cattle wandered all summer on seemingly endless BLM lease land, grazing with deer on
wild grass and occasionally losing calves to coyotes. Their round-
ups were just like on *Rawhide.*

At least I would have a horse, the talisman of the West and
the only way to get there. Television tempted me with satiny blond
palominos, powerful black thoroughbreds like Fury, startling
white stallions that reared up on their hind legs and pawed the air,
Hi ho Silver, away! My heart quickened to the *ta-da-dum, ta-da-
dum* of their hoofbeats as they galloped across the screen. I was as
dazzled as the first Indian watching the first white man ride up.
Here comes power and freedom and a way out.

My mother laughed at the idea. "You're too little for a horse," she said. "You'd just get trampled." I knew this was nonsense. For several weeks I had been sneaking off to Frank Chapman's pasture to ride the aging Percherons he couldn't bear to send to the glue factory. Frank called them Bob and Bill but I made up my own names: Quicksilver and Man O' War. I got them to come to me by shaking an old coffee can half-filled with grain; they couldn't resist the delicious rattle. Then I'd pick my steed by *eenie meanie minie*, lead it to the old tractor Frank had abandoned in a corner of the field, and scramble up the big back tire, keeping hold of my horse's halter. From there I could leap onto its broad back. The horse might snort and back away in surprise, but I stayed on, clinging to his tangled mane, thrilled. It didn't matter that my short legs stuck out on either side or that I could never get the horse to gallop no matter how hard I kicked. I was riding.

I would prove my mother wrong. One afternoon I opened Frank's pasture gate and led the horses out, pulling them along on some rotten strands of baling twine I'd found in the hayfield. My mother looked out her kitchen window to see us plodding up the road, the Percherons' huge heads on either side of mine, their hooves clip-clopping inches from my bare feet. She ran breathless into the yard. "Get over here!" she cried, and when we were close enough she snatched the twine away from me. The horses sensed her excitement and pulled back a little, dragging my mother along like she was weightless. *You're scaring them*, I said.

My mother let go of the twine and the old Percherons, feeling the sudden slack, turned and trotted back up the road, flinging their big heads in the air like colts. "No!" I shrieked, but she grabbed my arm and dragged me into the house while she called Frank. Luckily Man O' War and Quicksilver stopped to taste the grass growing thick around my father's fertilizer tank. They were still there, munching happily, when Frank drove up in his stock truck.

We used to hang horse thieves, he said to me as he climbed out of the cab, but he was smiling. He called to Bob and Bill and they came trotting up like two big old dogs. I watched him lead them up the ramp into his truck. My mother stood silently behind me, her hands gripping my shoulders.

"That's some kid you got there," he said to my mother, tousling my hair to show he wasn't mad. "Shoulda been a boy."

"I don't know what to do with her sometimes," my mother said. "She's just so darn strong willed."

I was only five years old, but I had heard this complaint many times before.

When he drove away she started in.

"What on earth were you thinking!" she scolded. "You could have been stepped on, even killed!" We both knew she was exaggerating.

"I want a horse," I said.

So my father bought a rangy buckskin gelding from a man he met at the salesyard. He got to talking to this cowboy sitting next to him and said he was looking for a gentle old saddle horse for his girl. *Well, I've got just the one*, Everett Watson grinned, showing a gap where his front teeth were missing. Everett and Maxine Watson ran a ranch up on the Salmon River but he even offered to haul it all the way to our farm for free. "That horse is way too cheap," my mother warned.

When Everett Watson backed the big gelding out of the trailer the horse kicked the side of it so hard I jumped. "Ole Buck here is a little nervous from the drive," Everett said, handing the lead rope to my father. "But he'll be just fine." He winked at me. I was so excited I could barely breathe. My father wrote Everett a check while I shifted from one foot to the other, itching to jump on Buck's back. "Put me on! Put me on!" I squealed, tugging on my father's arm.

The author's father, center front in dark jacket, at a horse auction, 1960

Maxine Watson got out of the truck and leaned against the door to roll herself a cigarette. She wore blue jeans and boots and a snap-button cowboy shirt like her husband and looked a little like Annie Oakley, except her hair was grey and her face all wrinkled. She put the cigarette in her mouth and lit a match with her fingernail, tossing it still burning into the road. Then she inhaled deeply and puffed out perfect smoke rings, the first time I had ever seen anyone do that. Maxine watched her smoke rings drift away and finally fall apart. *I sure hope he doesn't hurt her*, she said to nobody in particular.

How far can a father hear? Mine was turning water on the corn, clearing dirt clods out of the corrugates with the blade of his shovel, and I was in a pasture two fields away, chasing Buck. It had been several days since we got him and I had only ridden once, my feet dangling far above the stirrups of the old high-backed saddle Everett Watson let us have for five dollars more. Buck felt a lot different than Man O' War or Quicksilver, who patiently tolerated my weight and never even offered to nip when they took grain from my hand. This new horse had a way of bunching up his muscles and moving in a strange, hopping gait like a springed toy. For hours I rode Buck back and forth in front of the house, gripping the saddle horn with both hands when he jumped, refusing to get off even though my mother called through the kitchen window for me to come inside. "She's all right!" my father shouted back at her, grinning anxiously but determined to stand by his bargain.

I knew how to catch a horse with a can of grain, even if he was grazing in the middle of a big pasture. I knew my father was off somewhere irrigating and my mother was getting my brother to take a nap. Nobody to see and say no. So I got the grain and a piece of twine and went to find Buck. I was used to Quicksilver and Man O' War coming up to me, eager for food, but the minute I crawled under the pasture fence Buck trotted in the other direction, stopping now and then to pull up a mouthful of grass. I followed as close as I could, shaking the coffee can, calling *come here boy! have some grain!* but he kept maddenly out of my reach.

Finally I had him cornered in the V of two fencelines. I shook the can again, *here you go Buck!* and he turned his head to locate me, ears laid flat back. I ignored this unmistakable warning. I was concentrating so hard on where to grab his halter I didn't even see his hind foot flash out to catch me in the face, a perfect punch. I landed with a thud on the soft pasture grass and Buck reared up on his hind legs. *Just like Fury*, I thought hazily. Buck might have planted a hoof in my upturned face, but instead he jumped over me like a log. Lying on my back I watched the underside of his tawny body block out the sky, then slide away in slow motion. Was I underwater? I dimly heard hooves pounding the ground as he galloped away.

My father's rubber boots made a swishing sound in the grass, and then his big face was close to mine. "Are you all right sissie?" A big purple bruise spread across my cheek, over my temple, into my hair. He touched it lightly with a muddy finger and I flinched and started to cry. He sighed with relief. Not dead, at least. "Can you open your mouth honey?" I worked my jaw cautiously and a pain shot back into my ear. "It hurts!" I squealed, and he gathered me up in his arms and strode to the house, fear and rage and guilt making him even stronger. My mother had a cold washcloth ready when he put me down on the couch. She laid it on my cheek and held up three fingers, asked me how many, then looked into my eyes and felt my forehead for a fever, an automatic reflex. "Do you feel like throwing up?" she asked. She may have been a Christian Scientist, but she knew the medical symptoms of concussion. I shook my head and the pain made me gasp. *I'm gonna shoot that goddamned horse* my father growled, the first time I ever heard him swear. He turned and stomped into their bedroom, where he kept his guns. I heard him open the closet door.

"No!" I shouted, sitting up so suddenly the room swirled. "Don't kill Buck, please Daddy! Don't kill him!" I fell back on the couch, sobbing.

"Stop it!" My mother called sharply. "You're just upsetting her!"

Finally the closet door closed and he came back empty-handed and sat down beside me. He gazed at my swollen face and stroked my hair. His hand stopped and he pulled it back. His fingers were covered with a greenish goo. "You landed in a cow pie sis," he said, grinning. I wrinkled my nose and for some reason we all started laughing and couldn't stop. My brother stumbled in, clutching his ratty old stuffed bunny in one hand and rubbing his eyes with the other. All the noise woke him up. He stared at the three of us laughing like crazy and burst into tears.

My father took Buck to the salesyard the next Friday and sold him for practically nothing. For a week I got to lie on the couch, eat milk toast and drink Seven-Up, wonderful treats, but watching the cowboy shows was a torment. Silver and Trigger and Champion, even Dale Evans' gentle Buttermilk just reminded me that I had no horse. For once I was glad when Roy and Dale crooned "Happy Trails" and the afternoon cowboy shows gave way to re-runs of *The Little Rascals*. I was intent on my favorite episode, the one where the dog Petey sticks his tail in the gas chamber spout at the pound, when my mother came in with a fresh glass of soda. *It's too late, kids, your dog's dead*, the evil dog catcher crowed when the gang got there with the money to save Petey. The gang all started crying, but I gazed happily at the screen, waiting for the gas chamber door to open.

My mother knelt beside me and peered at my face. "Smile again," she commanded, and I obliged her strange request, stretching my mouth in a big false grin. She stared at my purplish-green cheek, shaking her head.

"That horse could have killed you," she said. "He could have knocked your teeth out, or broken your jaw. But all you got was a dimple! I can't wait for your father to see this." The gang was all hugging Petey now, shouting with delight. I held the foolish smile, forming my words through clenched teeth.

"Does this mean I can get another horse?"

The author and her brother at their uncle's house, 1955

Instead they sent me to first grade. When the teacher wasn't looking I drew ill-proportioned horses in my Big Chief writing tablet, right next to the lopsided hearts with Rex Lee's name inside. I longed alternately for a kiss from Rex or a new horse. Once I dreamed that my father bought me a caramel-colored palomino, complete with fancy bridle and saddle and a silver-studded martindale stretched across its powerful chest. It was so real I ran breathless in my nightgown into an empty yard. I even prayed to the Mormon Heavenly Father for a horse, though I suspected this was futile.

All it got me was an albino Shetland pony, foundered from eating too much grain. His owner was going to sell him for dog food but my father convinced the man to give us the colorless Shetland, ridiculously named Silver.

"He'll be good as new," my father said when he led Silver slowly out of his truck. I only scowled at this pitiful creature. Silver's hooves grew out like skis. It was all he could do to stumble painfully around the corral. For months my father kept his feet filed back and rubbed them with coal oil to help him heal, but Silver was a joke. My cousin Roger hooted with laughter, watching me trying to ride.

"Hi ho Sliver!" he shouted. I furiously kicked the crippled pony, but Silver could have been a statue of a horse for all the good he did me. When my father took Silver back to his owner I knew better than to ask what would happen to him.

It took a year of pleading to get another horse, a Morgan-quarterhorse mare named Bobby Socks because of her four white feet. The teenage girl who owned Bobby Socks had discovered boys, the mother said sadly, and that was the end of her horse-riding days. They needed to get rid of the horse to buy her a car. Bobby Socks was a beautiful auburn color, fast like a quarterhorse and muscular like a Morgan. Way too much horse for me, but we got a good deal. At least she didn't kick. I could catch her by myself and lead her back to the corral for my father to put the saddle on, then ride all over the farm, scaring up birds in the hayfields and humming the theme songs of my favorite cowboy shows. *Cheyenne. Lonely man.* I daydreamed of meeting Cheyenne Bodie, who was so tall and handsome and shy, and getting married and running a big cattle ranch together.

All summer Bobby Socks tolerated my absentminded riding but that fall we surprised some California pheasant hunters trespassing in the pasture and they shot over our heads for fun. Bobby Socks shied, ripping off my thumbnail where I held the reins, and then stretched out her neck like a racehorse, showing me the difference between a friendly gallop and a dead run. I yanked furiously on her reins but finally gave up and grabbed the saddlehorn with both hands, certain now that I would die. We thundered into the corral and just as it seemed she would smash into the fence she veered away, pitching me to the ground. Riderless and still terrified, Bobby Socks whirled and jumped the corral into Frank Chapman's pasture and kept going. The dangling reins snapped beneath her hooves. We found her the next day, her white stockinged legs all bloody from getting tangled in a downed barbed wire fence. Afterwards Bobby Socks hobbled around almost as bad as Silver and my father sold her at a loss, too. "We can't afford any more of this horse business," he said.

That was true until I wrecked our first new car, an absurdly finned, coral colored 1959 Chevrolet Biscayne my father left in gear and parked behind the truck the day my mother refused to take me to town. I wanted to go skating again at the "Rollaway," a big maple-floored rink where they played Elvis and Everly Brothers records and skating was almost like dancing. The junior high kids in town all went there. The rink smelled like the inside of shoes and Jade East shaving lotion and cigarette smoke, but it was heaven to me. A big ball covered with mirrors hung down from the ceiling, and when the lights dimmed it turned magically, sprinkling light on the skaters below. The cheerful disembodied voice of a disk jockey commanded us: "all skate!" "couples only!" or "ladies' choice!" My primary class had gone to the Rollaway the week before, a reward for memorizing *The Pearl of Great Price*. Skating around the darkened rink next to Mark Hansen, the mirror-ball casting glints of light on our solemn faces, the Everlys crooning "dream, dream, dream," was the most wonderful moment of my life so far. I was determined to re-create it, with Mark or one of the other cute boys I had seen at the rink.

The keys were always in the car. I knew enough to turn the ignition, but nothing about a clutch, and when the engine started the big Biscayne leaped forward. My foot searched frantically for the brake, pushing instead on the gas pedal. It took no more than a second to smash into the truck, but disasters happen in eerie slow motion when you're inside one. First the car made contact with the heavy truck bumper and nudged it forward a little. Then the Chevy's hood rippled like the surface of a pond, the waves rushing toward me, and my head fell forward and bounced off the steering wheel. Glass from the windshield cascaded inward, a waterfall of stinging shards. The driver's side door sprang open and I jumped out and was already in the yard by the time my father rushed outside to see what that terrible noise was. He stared aghast at his new car, crumpled up like so much tinfoil, and I threw myself on the ground.

"Don't kill me Daddy!" I screamed. "Don't kill me!"

He looked from me to the Chevy, too stunned to be angry. My mother stood me up and examined my face, the bloody nicks on my arms and legs. "I think she's okay," she said. I cowered, expecting my father to hit me for the first time in my life. But there are some things you do that your parents can't even imagine how to punish. We gaped in silence at the ruined car until finally I whispered hoarsely: *remember when you burned down the ranch house.*

"I'll call the insurance," my father muttered, his only words to me about it.

He told the insurance agent he was driving. Nobody would have believed a ten-year-old girl could do this. "How'd you get the shiner?" the agent asked me when he came out to inspect the damage. "Horse kicked her," my father said quickly. The Chevy cost $700 to fix, almost half of its new price, and my parents understood now what was the lesser of two evils. *Buy her another horse*, my mother said. *It will be cheaper in the long run.*

His name was Tony, a grey Arabian gelding from a dude ranch in the Sawtooths. Tony wasn't mean, his owner explained, just a little ornery and too damn smart. None of the dudes would

ride Tony because he'd brush them off on a fence, or stop in the middle of the trail and refuse to go any farther, or turn around and head for the barn.

"They can't make him go and they can't make him stop," the owner said. "What he needs is somebody he can't buffalo." My father talked about a price while I stroked Tony's smooth neck and rubbed him behind his ears. This time the horse was worth it. Tony and I were like Trigger and Roy, Champion and Gene, Silver and the Lone Ranger. We understood each other. The first time he balked I didn't sit there and kick him like a fool, I rubbed his neck and told him how much fun we would have up in the foothills, where it was so peaceful and empty. When I carelessly rode him into a snarl of barbed wire hidden in the grass he didn't panic. *Back up now boy*, I coaxed, barely pulling on the reins, and he stepped out of the deadly tangle as neatly as he walked in. So it was Tony who took me out far enough that I might find an arrowhead or imagine myself in the real West. It was Tony who found our way back when I wasn't paying attention and got us lost. When I was fourteen Tony bucked off my first real boyfriend and I couldn't help laughing. Tony stood placidly in the road, nodding his head happily. My humiliated ex-boyfriend picked himself up, stomped to his car, and barreled out of the driveway, drenching us in dust. *I know what you did*, I scolded him, but I had to smile.

Tony finally couldn't compete with our new Bel Aire. My father bought the shining white Chevrolet the summer after my horrible ninth grade year. Those long months were a nightmare I couldn't wake up from, a jumble of private dread and humiliation and a larger agony, my futile longing to be popular and hating PE and group showers all mixed up with President Kennedy getting shot and the whole horrible thing on television for days, replaying and replaying the instant his head blows apart, replaying and replaying the moment Lee Harvey Oswald feels the bullet burning into his guts, here's Mrs. Kennedy trying to get help, crawling across the trunk of the speeding limousine, John-John saluting the casket, the riderless horse.

I was in fourth period English when the principal's voice crackled over the intercom. *President Kennedy has been killed, Vice-President Johnson has been shot, and school is dismissed for the rest of the day.* At first some boys cheered and clapped for the dismissal part, but then they realized what else he said. The President was dead? Our English teacher Mrs. Broich was a good Catholic. For a long silent moment she glared at us. "I just hope the Russians aren't behind this," she said finally. "Or you all better have bomb shelters." Penny Kelly, a skinny little girl with a big bubble haircut, started crying hysterically. "Poor Jackie!" she wailed. Cynthia Larson, who wanted to be popular but was too tall, frowned and raised her hand. "Does this mean the noon sock hop is cancelled?" she asked. Cynthia loved to dance; she could do The Bird perfectly to "Wipe Out."

The long school bus ride home was eerily quiet. I prayed that the bombs wouldn't drop before I could get there. We listened to the radio reports about strange places that would become grimly familiar: Texas School Book Depository, Parkland Memorial Hospital, the grassy knoll. For once nobody yelled at the driver to turn to the Top 40 station.

The only thing good about ninth grade was driver's training in the spring. It was everybody's favorite class, even though the teacher pounded his fists on the dashboard and yelled every time a student made just a little mistake. Driving did not scare me. I knew how to steer our Massey-Ferguson tractor through narrow rows of bails; I had wrecked a car and lived. Finally I would be driving legally. My license was just for daytime, but that was enough.

The first time I drove alone was to Harold Russell's farm to pick up my father. He was helping Harold stack hay, but when they finished he couldn't get the pickup started. Someone needed to come get him. My mother was in the middle of freezing sweet corn, literally up to her elbows in sticky yellow kernels, when he called. This was my chance! The Russells lived farther west than any of our neighbors, just before the road dropped down and crossed the river into the next county.

"Can I go?" I pleaded, clenching my fists in excitement. "It's only a few miles. Can I?"

My mother looked from me to her kettles boiling on all four burners and back to me standing there so eager and thoughtless and terrifying. She knew this moment was inevitable. "I suppose," she sighed, and I was out of the house before she could tell me to be careful.

It was a glorious hot day. I rolled down my window and turned the radio up loud, to a new song by the Rolling Stones. Their lead singer was nowhere near as cute as Paul, but I liked them better than The Beatles. I hung my arm out the window and the summer air flowed over it like warm water. There was nobody else on the narrow county road. I pushed down on the gas pedal, watching the needle move through 50, 60, 70, flying past the turn-off to the Russell place. *I can't get no!* Mick Jagger screamed. Just ahead a stream of irrigation water rippled across the road, some careless farmer's runoff. It was wide, but shallow. In the distance I could see the smooth concrete bridge, the Payette River sparkling in the sun. I pushed the gas pedal down to the floor.

About the Author

ALICE KOSKELA was born in Council, Idaho, and spent the first year of her life on a mountain ranch near Lakefork. She lived her next sixteen years on a farm about midway between the southwestern Idaho farming communities of Emmett and New Plymouth. She attended a three-room grade school and graduated valedictorian. There were seven people in her class.

She has degrees from all three Idaho universities: a B.A. in English from Boise State University; an M.A. from Idaho State University; and a Juris Doctor from the University of Idaho. She wrote most of *The Pull of Moving Water* between 1995-1998, while attending law school.

She has been a high school and college English teacher, a newspaper reporter for the *Lewiston Morning Tribune,* a special assistant to former Governor Cecil D. Andrus, the statewide fundraiser for the Larry EchoHawk for Governor campaign, and a lobbyist for the Idaho Women's Network. She is now an attorney in Moscow, Idaho.

In 1994 she won the "Child Advocate of the Year" award from the Idaho Chapter of the American Society of Pediatrics. In 1995 she was awarded an Artist's Fellowship from the Idaho Commission on the Arts for an essay that metamorphosed into the first chapter of this book.

She lives in Moscow with her husband and son.